Jesu "Walk with Me."

*30 Days of Being With Jesus, Becoming
Like Jesus, and Doing Things with Jesus*

Copyright

Jesus Calls, "Walk With Me." © 2019 by David Milford.

Print Version   ISBN-13: 978-1-7337818-1-7

All Scripture Used With Permission

AMP

AMPC

CEV

ERV

Taken from the HOLY BIBLE: EASY-TO-READ VERSION ©
2001 by World Bible Translation Center, Inc. and used
by permission.

ESV

Scripture quotations are from the ESV® Bible (The
Holy Bible, English Standard Version®), copyright ©
2001 by Crossway, a publishing ministry of Good News
Publishers. Used by permission. All rights reserved.

EXB

Scripture taken from The Expanded Bible. Copyright
©2011 by Thomas Nelson. Used by permission. All
rights reserved.

GNT

Scripture quotations marked (GNT) are from the Good
News Translation in Today's English Version- Second
Edition Copyright © 1992 by American Bible Society.
Used by Permission.

ISV

The Holy Bible: International Standard Version is
Copyright © 1996-forever by The ISV Foundation. ALL
RIGHTS RESERVED INTERNATIONALLY.

KJV

The King James Version of the Bible is in the
public domain.

MSG

Scripture quotations marked MSG are taken from THE
MESSAGE, copyright © 1993, 1994, 1995, 1996, 2000,

2001, 2002 by Eugene H. Peterson. Used by permission of NavPress. All rights reserved. Represented by Tyndale House Publishers, Inc.

NASB

"Scripture quotations taken from the NASB. Copyright by The Lockman Foundation"

NIRV

Scripture quotations marked (NIrV) are taken from the Holy Bible, New International Reader's Version®, NIrV® Copyright © 1995, 1996, 1998, 2014 by Biblica, Inc.™ Used by permission of Zondervan. All rights reserved worldwide. www.zondervan.com The "NIrV" and "New International Reader's Version" are trademarks registered in the United States Patent and Trademark Office by Biblica, Inc.™

NIV

Scripture quotations marked (NIV) are taken from the Holy Bible, New International Version®, NIV®. Copyright © 1973, 1978, 1984, 2011 by Biblica, Inc.™ Used by permission of Zondervan. All rights reserved worldwide. www.zondervan.com The "NIV" and "New International Version" are trademarks registered in the United States Patent and Trademark Office by Biblica, Inc.™

NKJV

Scripture taken from the New King James Version®. Copyright © 1982 by Thomas Nelson. Used by permission. All rights reserved.

NLT

Names and details of stories have been changed in some instances to protect the privacy of the people involved.

Dedication

I dedicate this book to my nieces and nephews who will walk with Jesus in an intimacy I've dreamed about and chased after for over thirty years. I pray for you and your generation, that you may know Jesus in a way my generation never has.

I love you: Aidan, Alan, Alexis, Calvin, Chuck, Daisy, Danielle, Dean, Elijah, Ellen, Hayden, Jacob, Jayden, Jen, Joaquin, John, Kevin, Lauren, Lia, Logan, Lukas, Martin, Mat, Michelle, Mindie, Nate, Nathan, Randy, Sam, Sharon, William, and Yat Nam.

A Personal Note

Dear Friend,

Jesus Calls, "Walk With Me" is a 30-day journey into knowing and experiencing Jesus as a friend.

In 2009, I was embarrassed as I rode in the wheelchair that took me to my gate to board a plane. I was leaving Hong Kong after twelve years, going back to my hometown of Greenville, Pennsylvania. I could walk, but not far. Since then, I've had three surgeries (two hip replacements and foot surgery) and many procedures to my back for chronic pain from arthritis. God heals. I have prayed for hundreds of people and I have seen God do amazing healing miracles. I have His promise of healing. The only question is: "How will I handle the fire of a delayed answer to that promise?"

I discovered that constant pain swamped my days. Pain moved into my brain, overpowered my mind, and refused to leave. My days were a quagmire of pain, discouragement, and depression.

I began having extended times with Jesus every morning. I set no time limit. I stayed with Him until He lifted me above the pain. I learned to fight for each day. And over the last few years, I began to get parts of my life back. Joy rose up, and I was happy to have joy back in my life. Faith soared home and built a nest deep within. Peace reigned over some of my darkest days.

Something else was going on, something wonderful. I began having experiences with Jesus. He began to show me things. Most of all, He just loved me. And I changed. It's hard to describe how different life has been. Unable to run, run, run as I had all my life, I found Jesus in the stillness. Waiting for me. Wanting my friendship even more than I wanted His.

One day soon, I will be healed, and you can celebrate with me. In the meantime, here is the fruit the Holy Spirit has created in my life. I wouldn't trade my life for another, not for anything in the world. From the day I became a Christian in 1988, what I've desired most is to know Jesus, to really know Him and walk with Him the way Enoch walked with God. That desire took me to China, then Hong Kong. No matter where I've been, it has been the consuming passion of my life. And Jesus has not disappointed me.

With all my heart, I want you to know Jesus and walk with Him every day. As I have written this book, I have filled it with prayer for you, dear reader - that you will know Jesus as the friend, the good brother that He is. And the first thing He will do is take you to our Father.

In Christ,

Dave

Contents

Introduction – A New Paradigm - Changing the Way You See

> "Each of us tends to think we see things as they are, that we are objective. But this is not the case. We see the world, not as it is, but as we are – or, as we are conditioned to see it."
> -Stephen Covey[1]

I was in a prayer meeting in Hong Kong with a group that prayed together regularly. We got together every two weeks for ninety minutes of concerted prayer. We often heard God speaking to us, directing our prayers, and encouraging us. That day, however, God was silent. We prayed for a while, and kind of ran out of steam. It's hard to pray for a long time when you aren't hearing the Lord.

Finally, I cried out for God to speak to us. I felt He had withdrawn from us and I wondered what we had done wrong. I became desperate to hear His voice. I don't remember the exact words I prayed, but I asked Him to forgive us. I asked for His grace - His favor. I asked God to talk to us like He had been in these prayer times.

My friend, Jim, waited a few minutes. My words still hung in the air. Jim thanked God for the peace that had come over the room and told God how much he loved the sweet stillness we were experiencing. I heard others murmuring their agreement.

Huh? I opened my eyes and looked around. Others were at peace. I could see it on their faces.

---

[1] The 7 Habits of Highly Effective People; Powerful Lessons in Personal Change, Stephen R. Covey, 1989

What just happened? God was silent. Why did I perceive God's silence as disapproval and withdrawal while Jim and others found affirmation and approval in the same silence? I didn't have an answer that day, nor for many days to come.

I had a series of events over many months where I kept "discerning" what God was saying and doing as disapproval or correction. Others would interpret the same experience as something positive and affirming.

Something was wrong. I began to pray about it. What I discovered changed my life. I believe it will change yours too.

Perception Problems

From the moment we are born, we continuously try to understand what is going on in our lives. We notice things. We have experiences and make meaning from them. We build "knowledge" and understanding one piece at a time. We put things together. Over time, each of us develops ways of seeing things. *Paradigms.* A paradigm is the way we perceive, understand and make meaning of life. It's a mental map or model of our beliefs that explains reality.

Our minds are like computers in the sense that we have limited processing power. If we didn't have the ability to create paradigms (mental maps that explain complex things), we would constantly struggle to understand all the thousands of sensory impressions we receive every day. We perceive and interpret everything through the lens of our paradigms. Our paradigms influence how we see, feel, think and act.

Once we develop a paradigm, we rarely challenge its accuracy. We often aren't even aware of what our paradigms are. They are tools our minds use behind the scenes to deal with our complex world.

In fact, some of the paradigms that guide us all our lives were created when we were quite young. Sometimes, our paradigms are wrong. When that happens, our mental maps don't accurately represent reality. Like a flawed map, they won't take us where we need to go.

My experience with Jim in that prayer meeting and the series of events that followed made me question my paradigm for living a Christian life. Could my paradigm of Christianity be wrong? I honestly didn't know. In fact, I didn't know what my paradigm of Christianity was. I was about to find out.

God Placed Two Trees in the Garden

> Then the Lord God planted a garden in Eden in the east, and there he placed the man he had made. The Lord God made all sorts of trees grow up from the ground—trees that were beautiful and that produced delicious fruit. **In the middle of the garden, he placed the tree of life and the tree of the knowledge of good and evil.**
> Genesis 2:8-9 (NLT)

There were many trees in the garden, but only two are named: the tree of life and the tree of knowledge of good and evil. Did you notice that they were both in the center of the garden? These two trees represent the two basic paradigms of life. Each of us chooses one or the other. Our choice becomes the center of our thinking, the paradigm that we use to perceive, understand and make meaning of life. Our choice will determine how we see, feel, think and act.

The Tree of Knowledge of Good and Evil

> The serpent was the shrewdest of all the wild animals the Lord God had made. One day he asked the woman, "Did God really say you must not eat the fruit from any of the trees in the garden?"
>
> "Of course we may eat fruit from the trees in the garden," the woman replied. "It's only the fruit from the tree in the middle of the garden that we are not allowed to eat. God said, 'You must not eat it or even touch it; if you do, you will die.'"
>
> **"You won't die!"** the serpent replied to the woman. "God knows that your eyes will be opened as soon as you eat it, and **you will be like God, knowing both good and evil**."
>
> **The woman was convinced.** She saw that the tree was beautiful and its fruit looked delicious, and **she wanted the wisdom it would give her**. So she took some of the fruit and ate it. Then she gave some to her husband, who was with her, and he ate it, too. At that moment their eyes were opened, and they suddenly felt shame at their nakedness. So they sewed fig leaves together to cover themselves.
>
> When the cool evening breezes were blowing, the man and his wife heard the Lord God walking about in the garden. So they hid from the Lord God among the trees
>
> Genesis 3:1-8 (NLT)

Eve wanted to be like God. Eve didn't just disobey; she rebelled. She believed knowledge would elevate her, making her like God and she was willing to disobey to get it. Adam was there. He heard the conversation. He was silent. He ate the fruit too. *They dared to think that knowing what God knows would make them like God.*

You know the rest of the story. The serpent (Satan) lied. Adam and Eve died that day – spiritually. Their sin separated them from the life-giving relationship they had with God. And they discovered what God already knew. Life doesn't come from knowledge. Life comes only from a relationship with God.

The Tree of Life

Knowing God is life; separation from God is death.

> Eternal life means to know and experience you as the only true God, and to know and experience Jesus Christ, as the Son whom you have sent.
> John 17:3 (TPT)

> It is your ·evil [iniquity] that has separated you from your God.
> Isaiah 59:2 (EXB)

> Once you were dead because of your disobedience and your many sins.
> Ephesians 2:1 (NLT)

The tree of life is a relationship with God through Jesus. He is the way to God, the only way.

> Jesus answered, "I am ·the way, and the truth, and the life [or the one true way to have life].

> The only way to the Father is through me [L No one comes to the Father except through me].
> John 14:6 (EXB)

The first Adam chose the tree of knowledge. The second Adam, Jesus, chose the tree of life: the cross.

> The God of our fathers raised up Jesus whom you murdered by hanging on a tree.
> Acts 5:30 (NKJV)
> But Christ has rescued us from the curse pronounced by the law. When he was hung on the cross, he took upon himself the curse for our wrongdoing. For it is written in the Scriptures, "Cursed is everyone who is hung on a tree."
> Galatians 3:13 (NLT)

The goal of the tree of life (the relationship paradigm) is to be connected, living in union with Jesus. The relationship is everything. Life comes only through a relationship with Jesus – heart connection.

> My old identity has been crucified with Christ and no longer lives...
> ...Christ lives his life through me—**we live in union as one**!
> Galatians 2:20 (TPT)
> "I speak to you living truth: **Unite your heart to me and believe**—and you will experience eternal life!"
> John 6:47 (TPT)

Love empowers obedience. This isn't us trying to change ourselves. This is falling in love and letting love rule in our lives. This is being changed from the inside out.

> Jesus replied, "**Loving me empowers you to obey my word**. And my Father will love you so deeply that we will come to you and make you our dwelling place.
> John 14:23 (TPT)

A Vicious, Cruel Cycle

I was radical, sold out, living for God with everything I had. At 32, I had quit my job and left my townhouse-on-a-golf-course lawyer life in Tallahassee, Florida and gone to China to share Jesus. I held nothing back. I wanted a relationship with Jesus. I ran after Him with all my heart. I studied the Bible. I taught Bible studies. People began to come to me to help them understand the Bible and Christian life.

Yet, here I was, over a decade later, in Hong Kong, and I felt like I was treading water, floundering. At times my insecurity and defensiveness caused clashes with other Christians. I was focusing on my inadequacies and my failures. Tragically, when I looked at others what I noticed first was their inadequacies and missteps. This wasn't what I signed up for. Where was my love? Why was I so negative? Why couldn't I just enjoy people? Why couldn't I enjoy my own life?

I loved Jesus, and I knew His love. I had experienced amazing times with Him. I tried and tried to change myself. I failed again and again. It was a vicious, cruel cycle.

I didn't need to work harder or to try to have a more positive attitude. I needed a new paradigm.

Changing Paradigms

> "There are a thousand hacking at the branches of evil to one who is striking at the root."
> -Henry David Thoreau

The root of the way I saw myself and others, my feelings, my thinking and my behavior was a lie. A false paradigm. It was a lens that was distorting my perceptions, emotions, thoughts, and actions. In my zeal, I had made knowledge of the law of God my paradigm.

Everyone and everything was evaluated through this lens. I evaluated every sermon. Was that message right or wrong? I judged people. And myself. A knowledge paradigm reduces Christianity to a true/false test. I was constantly looking to find what was wrong with myself, others, my church... my life.

Like Adam and Eve, I dared to think that knowing what God knows would make me like God.

It didn't work for them, and it certainly wasn't working for me.

Finally, I saw what I was doing. That was the greatest breakthrough in my Christian life. When I changed my paradigm from knowledge (the law) to a relationship with Jesus, everything began to change. It wasn't an adjustment, it was a seismic shift – an earthquake!

> Jesus passionately cried out, took his last breath, and gave up his spirit.

At that moment the veil in the Holy of Holies was torn in two from the top to the bottom. **The earth shook violently, rocks were split apart, and graves were opened. Then many of the holy ones who had died were brought back to life and came out of their graves**. And after Jesus' resurrection, they were plainly seen by many people walking in Jerusalem.

Now, when the Roman military officer and his soldiers witnessed what was happening and **felt the powerful earthquake**, they were extremely terrified. **They said, "There is no doubt, this man was the Son of God!"**

Matthew 27:50-54 (TPT)

The law, the rules, and the principles that were from God still existed. But Jesus caused a seismic shift. The old ways were shaken.

"There is no doubt, this man was the Son of God!"

The law was the test. Jesus became the answer. The old way of principles, laws, and rules was superseded by a new way: relationship with Jesus. The way we see and interact with God changed. The temple curtain separating men from the presence of God was torn from the top down; Jesus gives us access to the presence of God. The law was replaced with something higher and infinitely more satisfying - a relationship with God through Jesus.

The old paradigm was God's truth, embodied in law and rules with harsh consequences. Harsh because sin meant death – separation from God. To be near, to live with God required purity, perfection. Blood sacrifices were made year after year for the sin of the people. The old paradigm was religion – the law. But man couldn't follow the law. Once that became abundantly clear, God revealed a new and better way.

The new paradigm is a person. Jesus. He became the once-for-all-time sacrifice. The new paradigm is love and grace – favor you don't deserve. The penalty for sin is death. Death is separation from life. This is life, to know and experience God through the way Jesus made for us. The new paradigm is relationship – family. And friends.

> Eternal life means to know and experience you as the only true God, and to know and experience Jesus Christ, as the Son whom you have sent.
> John 17:3 (TPT)

Paradigm shifts cause us to: see differently, feel differently, think differently, and act differently.

The thirty-day journey through this book will enable you to:

See differently. We tend to see what we look for. The knowledge paradigm keeps us looking at ourselves. And we are looking to judge. Is this right or is it wrong? If I look for what's wrong in myself and others, that's what I will see.

The knowledge paradigm elevates my soul (my will, mind, and emotions) to rule over my life. It's all about what I think, what I feel, my resolve and my self-discipline.

The relationship paradigm focuses on Jesus. My relationship with Jesus is my identity. My destiny is determined by my relationship with Jesus. This is the love paradigm. The driving question of my life becomes: "Have I learned to love?"

The love paradigm begins with my heart – my spirit. When the Holy Spirit comes into my heart, I can trust my heart and my spirit to lead me. This paradigm shift is a shift from mind (knowledge) to heart (relationship).

My spirit must rule over my soul (my mind, will, and emotions). The Holy Spirit comes inside me to lead me and make this earth-shaking paradigm shift. When the Holy Spirit leads, I can follow my heart. *My heart will take me places my mind can never go.*

You hear God. The Holy Spirit leads you. It's a heart thing.

> For all who are allowing themselves to be led by the Spirit of God are sons of God.
> Romans 8:14 (AMP)
> The true children of God are those who let God's Spirit lead them.
> (ERV)

You are a much-loved daughter or son. Follow your heart as the Holy Spirit leads in these devotions and activations. He will change your heart. He will teach you how to live through love.

Feel differently. When you start hearing Jesus clearly, it will be emotional. A lot of the pain you've lived with all your life is one experience with Jesus away from being blown to bits. Time after time, I've fallen before the Lord in awe and wonder as he has revealed Himself to me. I didn't know who I was until He showed me who

He is. He will do the same for you. And He will show you how he sees others, how he loves them, and you will begin to see others as He sees and feel what He feels.

> And I will give you a new heart—I will give you new and right desires—and put a new spirit within you. I will take out your stony hearts of sin and give you new hearts of love.
> Ezekiel 26:36 (TLB)

Think differently. New paradigms open new possibilities. Having a distorted or small vision of God limits us. Being with Jesus will renew your mind. That's how He changes us; He transforms us by changing the way we think.

> ...let God transform you into a new person by changing the way you think. Then you will learn to know God's will for you, which is good and pleasing and perfect.
> Romans 12:2 (NLT)
> ...be inwardly transformed by the Holy Spirit through a total reformation of how you think. This will empower you to discern God's will as you live a beautiful life, satisfying and perfect in his eyes.
> (TPT)

Act differently. Religion begins with behavior. Change this. Do that. It is demanding, hard and we fail again and again. All change that is real and lasting is heart change. It begins deep inside. The last evidence of heart change is what you do differently. And you do it because that is who you have become.

For as he thinks in his heart, so is he.

Proverbs 23:7 (NKJV)

> For it is [not your strength, but **it is] God who is effectively at work in you, both to will and to work [that is, strengthening, energizing, and creating in you the longing and the ability to fulfill your purpose]** for His good pleasure.
> Philippians 2:13 (AMP)

> For God is at work within you, helping you want to obey him, and then helping you do what he wants. (NLT)

> Jesus replied, "Loving me empowers you to obey my word. And my Father will love you so deeply that we will come to you and make you our dwelling place.
> John 14:23 (TPT)

How to Use this Book - A Vision to Empower Your Race

> "...let us run with endurance the race He has set before us."
> Hebrews 12:1 (NIV)

This book is broken into 31 readings.

Introduction – **A New Paradigm** – Changing the Way You See

God Has a **Plan**. (Days 1-2)

God's Plan Begins with a **Person** – Jesus. (Days 3-4)

Jesus Made a **Path** for You. (Days 5-6)

The Path is a **Process**.

1. **Be With Jesus** (Days 7-14)

2. **Become Like Jesus** (Days 15-22)

3. **Doing Things With Jesus** (Days 23-30)

I offer this simple framework as a solid foundation for your relationship with Jesus. The heart of our walk with Jesus is being with Him, becoming like Him, and doing things with Him. This process will keep you focused on Him and bring balance and strength to your life.

Be With Jesus

God wants people to look at us and know that we are someone who spends time with Jesus. While living in Beijing and Hong Kong, I met some spiritual giants. I've met people who walk into a room and the atmosphere changes. They have been to the secret place. They are friends of Jesus. And He tells them secrets. When they share, you know the Lord is speaking. The presence of God is radiating from them. They are great lights for the Lord. That is God's plan for you and me – each of us and all of us. Days 7-14 take you to meet with Jesus.

Become Like Jesus

I've met Christians from all walks of life who have such sweetness of spirit. My wife is one of them. I'm inspired to know that people can be living examples of the gentle goodness of Jesus. One of my favorite people on the planet is a humble fishmonger in Hong Kong. His life is hard, but the joy of the Lord on this precious servant lifts up everyone around him. His life is Jesus' message, written on a human heart. He is a brilliant light whose hope and joy are contagious. I'm smiling just thinking about him.

We will most effectively change our world when people look at us and see something they really want, but don't have. Days 15-22 show you how to let the Holy Spirit change you to become like Jesus.

Do Things With Jesus

I love spending time with friends who are always up for an adventure. They walk with Jesus every day. And whatever He asks, they do. Because they can be trusted, Jesus gives them assignments. He has adventures for you too.

One of these precious friends went with us to the hospital where my wife's mother was in a diabetic coma. It was late at night. In the waiting room outside the critical care unit, we met a family whose grief and despair were heart-wrenching. I have rarely seen such hopelessness. Mark immediately went to comfort them. Mark prayed for their family member in critical care. He brought hope to their hearts, and two of them gave their lives to Jesus in the middle of the night outside that critical care unit. Next, we prayed for my mother-in-law. The Lord told my wife she would recover. She did. My mother-in-law lived for several years after this. Days 23-30 are written to launch you on your personal adventures with Jesus.

I. A Plan – God's Plan for You

Your first child is born. You reach out to hold her for the first time. So tiny. So fragile. So helpless. You adjust your trembling hands to support her neck. Oh, my! Look at her little fingers. You study her. She has your nose, poor girl. But her mother's eyes. You smile. At that moment, you are in awe of the gift of life. In your hands, you cradle all the possibilities, all the potential of a new human life. You didn't know you could love someone this much. You are overwhelmed with joy yet in awe of the responsibility. You hold her to your chest, your heart beating with hers. This is, without a doubt, the best day of your life.

That's how God felt when you were born. He imagined you. He lovingly crafted you. He placed you in the time, place and family He had prepared for you. Your parents may not have wanted you. God did. God created you because He wanted you to be His.

Knowing God's plan for you will answer the two most significant life questions each of us asks: Who am I? And what is the meaning, the purpose of my life?

Identity.

You are a greatly loved daughter or son of God. That's who you are. Family is God's idea. And He wants you to live as His son, His daughter - that close, that cherished. God's fatherly love for you defines you.

"Who is that guy?"

"God's son."

"Wow! I knew he was somebody."

Meaning and Purpose of Life.

God is the ruler, the Lord of all that is. His sons and daughters are royalty. He told Adam and Eve to fill the earth and have dominion over it – rule it. God's plan hasn't changed. He wants us to establish the kingdom of God on the earth. Each of us has specific assignments, things God has planned for us to do. The meaning of life is to take our place and influence our world with the love of God.

Day 1 Jesus Calls, "How Well Do You Know Dad?"

"And I will be a father to you, and you shall be sons and daughters to Me," Says the Lord Almighty.

2 Corinthians 6:18 (NASB)

See how very much our Father loves us, for he calls us his children, and that is what we are! But the people who belong to this world don't recognize that we are God's children because they don't know him.

1 John 3:1 (NLT)

The Spirit you received does not make you slaves so that you live in fear again; rather, the Spirit you received brought about your adoption to sonship. And by him we cry, "Abba, Father." The Spirit himself testifies with our spirit that we are God's children.

Romans 8:15-16 (NIV)

Daddy

Several years ago, Karen, my wife, and I were walking with her parents to meet the rest of the family at a restaurant in Hong Kong for our weekly family dinner. As we began to walk, Daddy Chan reached out and took my hand.

The whole world stopped for me at that moment.

I felt four years old again. Daddy held my hand. I felt so loved by the wonderful man who was my wife's father. Daddy and I had never had a conversation without an interpreter; my Cantonese was that bad. But he loved me. And I loved him, and it was enough for both of us.

The walk to the restaurant was far too short for me. As I felt the pressure of Daddy's hand on mine, I began to understand God's love in a way that my mind never could. I held back the tears as my heart filled with God's Fatherly love.

I had felt God's presence before, but not like this. I had been taught that God was distant and I was unworthy. Those beliefs were shattered in an instant as I experienced God's love through the gnarled hand of my wife's dear father.

> "And you will know the truth, and the truth will set you free."
> John 8:32 (NLT)

Ginōskō is the Greek word "know" in this verse. It means: **"to know, especially through personal experience (*first-hand* acquaintance)."**[2]

I knew that God loved me. I could quote the scriptures. Yet I still prayed striving prayers. I still struggled to somehow be found worthy of intimacy with God. I so wanted to be like Enoch, the man who walked with God. Enoch pleased God. Imagine that. Deep in my heart, I believed I wasn't good enough to be loved like that.

When Daddy took my hand, I felt God's love in a way I can't explain. I didn't expect it. I didn't deserve it. And that was God's point. He loved me. And I knew God wanted to walk with me the same way Daddy was walking with me.

I walked hand-in-hand with Daddy several times after that. Daddy went home to the Lord a few years later. I treasure the memory of those walks. I'll always remember Daddy Chan's gnarled hand, gold-toothed smile, and that day when Daddy took my hand and God changed my life.

The Experience of Knowing God

It's not enough to know about God with our minds. Our hearts will take us places our minds can never go. Jesus invites us to ginōskō (to know) His Father as our Father.

> Eternal life means **to know and experience you as the only true God**, and **to know and**

---

[2] Strong's Exhaustive Concordance: New American Standard Bible. Updated ed. La Habra: Lockman Foundation, 1995. http://www.biblestudytools.com/concordances/ strongs-exhaustive-concordance/.

> **experience Jesus Christ**, as the Son whom
> you have sent.
> John 17:3 (TPT)

The Greek word translated "know and experience" here is – yes, you guessed it - ginōskō. God's plan from the beginning was to have human children and walk with them. The picture of Adam and Eve walking with God in the cool of the evening is what God wanted to do with each of us. He still does. Jesus came to make God's dream come true.

Your new life begins as you come to know God through experiences with Him. This is no religion. This is no mind thing. It's not cold, hard facts. It's a warm, loving relationship. It's real. It's powerful. It's everything you ever hoped life would be. Open your heart. In the next 30 days, Jesus is going to take you on an adventure into the heart of God.

Activation

You may know that God wants to be part of your life. But hearing it from Him makes all the difference. So, ask Him. I realize that may not be what you are used to, so let's do this in simple steps.

Knowing Father's Voice

The steps here are based on Dick Eastman's book *The Purple Pig and Other Miracles*[3] and my personal experiences.

1. **God still speaks to people today.**

---

[3] The Purple Pig and Other Miracles, Dick Eastman, page 108

The Bible makes scripture come alive. The Bible is the Holy Spirit talking to us. See Day 8 Jesus Calls, "Meet Me in My Word." In the Bible (e.g., 1 Kings 19) we learn that God sometimes talks to us in a "still, small, voice." To many, this is a "heart impression" or an "inaudible voice."

To hear God, you need to believe that God speaks to people today.

2. **God speaks from His dwelling place, the hearts of His children**.

The Holy Spirit lives in us once we are born again. So, it is only natural we would hear Him within ourselves.

> "...I will ask the Father, and he will give you another Advocate, who will never leave you. He is the Holy Spirit, who leads into all truth. The world cannot receive him, because it isn't looking for him and doesn't recognize him. But you know him because he lives with you now and later will be in you." John 14:16–17 (NLT)

When Jesus died and was resurrected, Christians received the Holy Spirit to live in us.

> "Do you not know that you are the temple of God and that the Spirit of God dwells in you?" 1 Corinthians 3:16 (NKJ)

What is it like when God speaks to us? We all have a running dialog in our heads. When it is from God "it is a quiet thought or impression that flows out of one's heart and into his or her mind."[4]

---

[4] Eastman, p 106

3. **God gives us the privilege and the responsibility of hearing His voice.**

> "My sheep listen to my voice; I know them, and they follow me."
> John 10:27 (NLT)

The Bible is very clear on this point. Those who follow Jesus, hear His voice.

4. **Silence other voices.**

There are three voices we can hear in our heads: our own voice, Satan's, and God's.

Our path to silencing other voices is found in James: "Submit yourselves, then, to God. Resist the devil, and he will flee from you." James 4:7 (NIV)

Submit yourselves to God. True submission will silence "self."

Resist the devil, and he will flee from you. The Bible gives us authority over the devil. Take it.

Pray, *"Lord, it's not what I want here. I submit to Your will. Satan, be quiet. Lord, I only want to hear Your voice."*

5. **Does it sound like Jesus?**

Everything Jesus or the Father say to you will be consistent with the Bible and Jesus' character and heart.

Day 12 Jesus Calls, "Train Your Heart to Listen When I Speak." explains in more detail how to hear God's voice with confidence.

Ready?

Ask God, "Father God, how do You want me to experience You today?"

What did He say? Treasure God's words to you. Write them down. You will find that, over time, God will show you big things from the short, daily messages He gives you. You will see patterns and the pieces will fit together.

One word from God changes everything. The Christian life is heart connection with God through Jesus. God hears you. He wants you to hear Him. Then you will come to know Him as your Father.

Day 2 Jesus Calls, "Dad Wants You to influence the Earth."

There's a story every person on the planet needs to hear. This story answers the two great questions all of us ask at some point in our lives: *Who am I?* and *What is the meaning and purpose of my life?* The story is a little long as it covers thousands of years. Here is a short version.

God created Adam and Eve to be His children. He wanted a family. I'm not entirely sure why. But I believe God just saw great joy in having human children. He made Adam in His image, and from Adam He created Eve. They were like Him because fathers want their children to be like them.

Like all good parents, God gave his children responsibility to help them grow up. Children born into a royal family are taught responsibility by giving them parts of the kingdom to rule for the king. God told Adam and Eve to multiply, to fill the earth, and subdue it – rule over everything on earth.

> God blessed them and said to them, "Be fruitful and increase in number; fill the earth and **subdue it**. **Rule** over the fish in the sea and the birds in the sky and over every living creature that moves on the ground."
> Genesis 1:28 (NIV)
> … what are mere mortals that you should think about them, human beings that you should care for them? Yet you made them only a little lower than God and crowned them with glory and honor. **You gave them charge of**

> **everything you made, putting all things under their authority....**
> Psalms 8:4-6 (NLT)

Love Ruled the Earth

Have you ever wondered what Adam, Eve, and the world were like before Satan got his hands on them? Created things reflect their creator. God is love. Imagine the earth filled with only the goodness of God – nothing else. I believe this scripture gives us a glimpse of what life was like when love ruled the earth:

> Those who are loved by God, let his love continually pour from you to one another, because God is love. Everyone who loves is fathered by God and experiences an intimate knowledge of him. The one who doesn't love has yet to know God, for God is love.
> 1 John 4:7-8 (TPT)

The dominion over the earth that God gave to man was love. In God's kingdom, rulers serve.

> "The kings and men of authority in this world rule oppressively over their subjects... But this is not your calling. You will lead by a different model. **The greatest one among you will live as one called to serve others without honor. The greatest honor and authority is reserved for the one who has a servant heart.**
> Luke 22:25-26 (TPT)

God's plan for Adam, Eve and all His children was to be in a life-giving relationship with Him, to be loved, and to love. To help them grow, God gave his children authority and responsibility: fill the earth and rule over it for God.

There's A Snake in the Garden

Satan (Lucifer), the angel who wanted to be like God, led a rebellion of one-third of the angels in heaven. The good angels defeated them and God threw Satan and the rebellious angels out of heaven. Satan and his defeated army tumbled to the earth. (See Revelation 3:9-12)

> "How you are fallen from heaven, O Lucifer....
> For you have said in your heart: 'I will ascend
> into heaven, I will exalt my throne above the
> stars of God.... **I will be like the Most High**.'
> Yet you shall be brought down to Sheol, to the
> lowest depths of the Pit.
> Isaiah 14:12-15 (NKJV)
> He [Jesus] replied, "I saw Satan fall like lightning
> from heaven.
> Luke 10:18 (NIV)

Satan came to Eve disguised as a snake. He told Eve she would become like God if she ate the fruit God said not to eat. God had warned Adam and Eve not to eat that fruit, or they would die. Satan scoffed, "Surely you won't die." Eve really wanted to be like God. She ate the fruit. Adam listened to Eve and ate the fruit. They died that day – spiritually. Their disobedience broke their life-giving connection with God. And without realizing what they had done, they gave Satan their authority over the earth God had given them to rule for Him.

> Don't you realize that you become the slave
> of whatever you choose to obey? You can

> be a slave to sin, which leads to death, or
> you can choose to obey God, which leads to
> righteous living.
> Romans 6:16 (NLT)

Now, the whole world came under Satan's control.

> We know that we are children of God, and that
> the whole world is under the control of the
> evil one [Satan]
> 1 John 5:19 (NIV)

Thousands of years later, Satan bragged to Jesus that
the whole world was his; it had been given to him. Jesus
didn't argue because it was true.

> The devil led him [Jesus] up to a high place and
> showed him in an instant all the kingdoms of
> the world. And he said to him, "I will give you all
> their authority and splendor; **it has been given
> to me, and I can give it to anyone I want to.** If
> you worship me, it will all be yours."
> Luke 4:5-8 (NIV)

God had given, irrevocably, all authority over the earth
to Adam and Eve. They gave it to Satan. If the earth
and mankind would ever overthrow Satan's cruel
government, a man would have to overcome Satan.

A Man Stands Up to Satan

Jesus was that man. He was God's son born to a woman.
Everything Jesus did on earth He did as a man. God led,
empowered, and helped Jesus the same way He does us
– through the Holy Spirit. Jesus, the man, empowered
by the Holy Spirit, did not sin.

Satan influenced men to betray and kill Jesus. Death, the result of man's disobedience (sin) could not hold Jesus because he never sinned.

The Holy Spirit brought Jesus back to life. And in a stunning turnaround, God pronounced sentence on Satan for the murder of Jesus. God proclaimed that Jesus' death would pay the price for the disobedience of all men. Men could receive forgiveness and be restored as God's sons and daughters if they chose to make Jesus savior and lord of their lives.

> For God made Christ, who never sinned, to be the offering for our sin, so that we could be made right with God through Christ.
> 2 Corinthians 5:21 (NLT)

God's Family is Restored

1. **Your Identity**

When you were born again, you were born into God's kingdom as a daughter, a son. Your Dad is the king. You are family. And you are royalty. That's who you are.

> But to all who believed him and accepted him, he gave the right to become children of God.
> John 1:12 (NLT)
> You are now children of God because you have put your trust in Christ Jesus.
> Galatians 3:26 (NLV)
> But you are a chosen people, **a royal priesthood**, a holy nation, a people belonging to God, that you may declare the praises of him who called you out of darkness into his wonderful light.

1 Peter 2:9 (NIV)

"You have made them to be a **kingdom [of royal subjects] and priests to our God**; and **they will reign on the earth**."
Revelation 5:10 (AMP)

2. The Meaning and Purpose of Your Life

God took all authority over the earth from Satan and gave it to Jesus. By faith, we walk in Jesus' authority as we walk in relationship with Jesus.

> Then Jesus came to them and said, "**All authority in heaven and on earth has been given to me.** Therefore go and make disciples of all nations..."
> Matthew 28:18 (NIV)
> And he alone is the leader and source of everything needed in the church. **God has put everything beneath the authority of Jesus Christ** and has given him the highest rank above all others. **And now we, his church, are his body on the earth** and that which fills him who is being filled by it!
> Ephesians 1:22-23 (TPT)

We have seen "authority" abused all over the earth. God's kingdom authority doesn't look anything like your angry boss, bullying teacher or the controlling stepparent in your life.

The Merriam Webster Dictionary defines **authority**: *power to influence or command thought, opinion, or behavior.*5

---

[5] Merriam Webster online dictionary

Leaders in God's kingdom are servants. God gives us His authority to influence the earth. Love is the authority God gives us. We take authority over the devil and demons by force, in Jesus name. We influence people by loving them with Jesus' love.

God has given you the power to influence the thoughts, beliefs, and actions of others with His love – love that this world so desperately needs. God has specific plans for you to influence your world.

> This is why God selected and ordained us to be his own inheritance through our union with Christ! Before we were even born, he gave us our destiny; that we would fulfill the plan of God who always accomplishes every purpose and plan in his heart.
> Ephesians 1:11 (TPT)

What are God's specific plans for you? That's the adventure, my friend. He planned in advance your destiny and the specific things that you would do. Ask Him. And start walking with Jesus.

Activation

Father, you made me as a unique expression of Yourself. I was born to be part of Your loving family. And I was born to live a life of influence. You have specific things planned for me to do with my life. I want to do them, all of them.

Ask Him: "Jesus, who do you want me to touch today with Father's love?"

Listen. Then do what He says. I do this every morning. He always has someone I know who needs something only He can give. It's a great way to influence your world.

II. A Person

His birth was announced in the stars. Only a few wise men followed the stars to Bethlehem. Angels broke out in song, announcing His arrival, but only shepherds saw them. His father was God. His mother was a common woman named Mary. His name was Jesus.

News like this could not be kept secret long. Now, an epic battle began; the struggle for the spiritual lives of all men who would ever live.

Day 3 Jesus calls, "Few Things are Needed. Really, Only One."

David obsessed about one thing: being with God, being in His presence.

> **One thing have I asked of the Lord**,
>
> that will I seek, inquire for, and [insistently] require:
>
> **that I may dwell in the house of the Lord [in His presence] all the days of my life**,
>
> to behold and gaze upon the beauty [the sweet attractiveness and the delightful loveliness] of the Lord and to meditate, consider, and inquire in His temple.
>
> Psalm 27:4 (AMPC)

In one of the most amazing stories in the Bible, God broke the rules so David could be with Him. Do you know the story?

God told Moses to build a tabernacle so God's presence could be with the people during their journey from Egypt to the Promised Land. God gave Moses detailed plans. Everything had to be done exactly as God commanded. Moses had the tabernacle built. The Ark of the Covenant, where the presence of God dwelt, was placed in the innermost court, the Holy of Holies. The glory of God fell upon the tabernacle and stayed there, day and night for over forty years while the Israelites were in the desert.

> **Then the cloud covered the tent of meeting, and the glory of the Lord filled the tabernacle**. Moses could not enter the tent of meeting because the cloud had settled on it, and the glory of the Lord filled the tabernacle.
>
> In all the travels of the Israelites, whenever the cloud lifted from above the tabernacle, they would set out; but if the cloud did not lift, they did not set out—until the day it lifted. **So the cloud of the Lord was over the tabernacle by day, and fire was in the cloud by night**, in the sight of all the Israelites during all their travels.
>
> Exodus 40:34-38 (NIV)

Imagine that. Every morning you could go out of your tent, look at the tabernacle tent, and see proof that God was with you that day - the tangible, supernatural presence of God.

When Israel finally arrived in the Promised Land, the tabernacle was placed at Shiloh in Samaria where it remained for 400 years. Then the Israelites risked and lost the Ark of the Covenant when they took it into battle against the Philistines. God allowed them to be defeated because of their sin. (1 Samuel 4).

The glory of God left the tabernacle when the Ark of the Covenant was removed. The priests continued making sacrifices there, but they were just going through the motions. God's glory remained on the Ark of the Covenant.

The Philistines placed the ark in the temple of their god, Dagon. In the morning, the huge statue of Dagon had fallen on its face. They set Dagon upright. The next morning, Dagon had fallen again before the ark of the covenant of God, the statue's head and hands had broken off. (1 Samuel 5) God punished the Philistines with a series of plagues. The Philistines wisely returned the Ark of the Covenant to Israel with gifts of gold as offerings for their sin against God. (1 Samuel 6)

The ark was left at Beth-shemesh. Seventy men from Beth-shemesh died when they opened and looked into the ark. In great fear, the people of Beth-shemesh asked the people of Kiriath-jearim take it away. For seventy years the ark remained at Kiriath-jearim, just five miles from Gibeon where the Tabernacle of Moses stood. No one dared to move it.

David longed for the presence of God. He decided to move the ark. With great joy, praising and making music with lyres, harps, symbols, trumpets, and tambourines they placed the ark on an ox cart and began the eight-mile trip to bring the Ark to Jerusalem. The oxen stumbled. Uzzah reached up to steady the ark. When he touched it, he died. David was angry, then afraid. He left the ark at a farmer's home and asked God how to move it.

David's idea from the first was not to move the ark to the Tabernacle of Moses, but to a different tabernacle he had made. Only the high priest could go into the presence of God, the holy of holies in the Tabernacle of Moses, and then only once a year. David created a tabernacle where priests, trained as musicians and singers, and David, himself, could go into God's presence and praise and worship Him. Finally, David moved the Ark.

Scripture doesn't say this was God's idea. It was in David's heart, and God let David do it. David established continuous praise and worship in the presence, the glory of God. I wonder how many of the Psalms were written or received from God during praise and worship in the tabernacle of David.

David asked for "one thing." He risked his life to get it. God broke the rules He gave to Moses, to fulfill David's heart desire:

> I ask only one thing, Lord: Let me live in
> your house every day of my life to see how
> wonderful you are and to pray in your temple.
> Psalm 27:4 (CEV)

Passion and Purpose

Paul writes eloquently about the passion that overwhelms him and the purpose he had found as he pursued Jesus. All his life before Jesus counted for nothing. Knowing Jesus was everything to Paul.

> My beloved ones, **don't ever limit your joy or fail to rejoice in the wonderful experience of knowing our Lord Jesus!**

Yet all of the accomplishments that I once took credit for, I've now forsaken them and **I regard it all as nothing compared to the delight of experiencing Jesus Christ as my Lord**! To truly know him meant letting go of everything from my past and throwing all my boasting on the garbage heap. It's all like a pile of manure to me now, so that I may be enriched in the reality of knowing Jesus Christ and embrace him as Lord in all of his greatness.

Philippians 3:1, 7 (TPT)

Deuteronomy 4:24 says that our God is a "consuming fire, a jealous God." I've found my relationship with Jesus is like that. He grows greater in my heart, consuming distractions and rivals for my affection. His love overwhelms me and draws me nearer.

My passion is to be consumed with him and not clinging to my own "righteousness" based in keeping the written Law. My "righteousness" will be his, based on the faithfulness of Jesus Christ—the very righteousness that comes from God. **And I continually long to know the wonders of Jesus more fully and to experience the overflowing power of his resurrection working in me.** I will be one with him in his sufferings and I will be one with him in his death. Only then will I be able to experience complete oneness with him in his resurrection from the realm of death.

Philippians 3:9-11 (TPT)

Paul left everything behind to follow Jesus: his family, his friends, his mentor (the great rabbi and

Sanhedrin leader, Gamaliel), his career ambitions and his reputation. He went from being a hero of the Jews to one despised and persecuted by the very people who used to adore him. They beat him repeatedly and tried to stone him to death. Looking back, Paul said everything that had meant so much to him before he met Jesus was now worthless, like manure to him.

Thirty years ago, I asked Jesus to save me. He did. He rescued me from an alcoholic hell I can't even imagine now – it was so dark, so hopeless. I heard Him calling me to "one thing." I committed then, and hundreds of times since then to live my life for "one thing." My life is not my own. Jesus bought me with His life. I live for one thing: Jesus.

I quit my job as a lawyer, sold my townhouse on a golf course, and moved around the world a year after I became a Christian. I went to China for one thing: to get closer to Jesus. I went to serve Him and the people of China. Jesus met me in China. I am wrecked. Nothing else satisfies. Only Him. Always Him.

So, He comes. Morning after morning, Jesus meets with me. He talks to me. He walks with me throughout the day. Early on in my Christian life, I envied Enoch because he walked with God. Now, I know that every person who makes Jesus the Savior and Lord of their lives can walk with Jesus.

Activation

Make Jesus the ONE THING in your life.

> "Martha, Martha," the Lord answered. "You are worried and upset about many things. But **few things are needed. Really, only one thing is**

needed. Mary has chosen what is better. And it will not be taken away from her."

Luke 10:41-42 (NIRV)

The "one thing" Mary chose was to sit at the feet of Jesus.

I pray the fiery passion of God will fall on you, that you won't be satisfied with anything less than knowing and walking with Jesus every day of your life. And in that passionate relationship, you will find your purpose in life and the contentment that comes only from being with Jesus.

> **So let all who are fully mature have this same passion, and if anyone is not yet gripped by these desires, God will reveal it to them**.
>
> Philippians 3:15 (TPT)

Tell Him your decision in your own words.

Day 4 Jesus Calls, "I Complete You."

> So now the case is closed. There remains no
> accusing voice of condemnation against those
> who are joined in life-union with Jesus, the
> Anointed One.
> Romans 8:1 (TPT)

Who Do You Think You Are?

For seven years I was part of a biweekly prayer meeting
at a church in Hong Kong. That prayer meeting was
an incubator. Each of us was learning how to pray.
We were also learning who God is and who we are. In
the midst of prayer battles, we learn a lot about God
and ourselves.

One of the most important lessons came from several
times where our prayer sessions began with someone
agonizing about how inadequate we were.

"O, Lord, I am just a worm! We fail you, God.
Forgive us."

Others jumped into the pit. The more they confessed
their feelings, the deeper we sank. Our focus shifted
from God to ourselves and, flailing in the pit of
condemnation, we lost our way. Guilt and shame
wrecked those prayer meetings. These were good
people – dedicated warriors who loved Jesus, yet didn't
feel worthy to approach Him. Some of those prayer
meetings never recovered. We prayed for an hour and a
half and never got out of that pit.

If you have asked Jesus to forgive your sin and have
made Him your Savior and Lord, Jesus took your guilt to

the cross, enduring the shame, for the joy of setting you free. Your life is joined in "life union with Christ." "There remains no accusing voice of condemnation" against you. Romans 8:1.

Yet we hear a voice of condemnation. Even mature Christians who live wholeheartedly for Jesus hear that voice. Satan is the accuser. It's his voice you are hearing. Ignore Him. He is a liar.

Before you will feel comfortable walking with Jesus in a real, personal way, you need to accept that Jesus' death on the cross perfects you so you can boldly approach God. You need to know God as a loving Father. And you need to know your human frailty doesn't disqualify you from walking side by side with Jesus.

Jesus paid a terrible price to set you free from the crippling wounds of condemnation, guilt, and shame. Don't go back into Satan's pit!

> So now there is no condemnation for those who belong to Christ Jesus. And because you belong to him, the power of the life-giving Spirit has freed you from the power of sin that leads to death.
>
> Romans 8:1-2 (NLT)
>
> Therefore let us [with privilege] approach the throne of grace [that is, the throne of God's gracious favor] with confidence *and* without fear, so that we may receive mercy [for our failures] and find [His amazing] grace to help in time of need [an appropriate blessing, coming just at the right moment].
>
> Hebrews 4:16 (AMP)

I love Hebrews 4:16. We have the privilege of approaching God's throne. It is a throne of grace for us who believe and obey. We approach God with confidence, without fear, knowing we will receive mercy for our failures and help in time of need.

When God Looks at You, What Does He See?

I know you sin from time to time. I wish I could say I didn't, but I do too. So how can you or I boldly approach God who is holy and who will not ever compromise with sin?

God sees you through Jesus' performance, not yours.

> But **our High Priest offered himself to God as a single sacrifice for sins, good for all time**. Then he sat down in the place of honor at God's right hand. ... For by that one offering **he forever made perfect those who are being made holy**.
> Hebrews 10:12, 14 (NLT)

When God looks at you, he sees you through Jesus' single sacrifice (his life for ours). Jesus "forever made perfect those who are being made holy." That's who you are! Your daily performance has nothing to do with that. Jesus' sacrifice was once for all time. His forgiveness is continuous, never-ending.

How does Conviction Differ from Condemnation?

I was in China from 1989-1992. I loved China so much. I thought I would be there all my life. In January 1992, I was rushed to a hospital in Beijing with what appeared to be a heart attack. My pain increased with no progress in the diagnosis or treatment for sixteen days. Friends finally convinced me to leave. I was flown to Hong Kong where I was admitted to a hospital. I had a bleeding ulcer. In defeat, I finally went home to Pennsylvania, a very sick man.

Six months later, I was still regaining strength. My ulcer had not yet healed, but I wanted to go back to China. I began to pray. For three years, I prayed fervently to God. Send me back to China. The answer was, "No." I kept praying, asking, and then pleading. Finally, I was arguing with God. Yeah, I know.

One night, I was crying out, "Why Lord? Why? Why can't I go back to China?" I raised my voice, "Why?"

In the loudest voice, I've ever heard the Lord use, He said, "It's the wrong question!"

I fell on my face on the floor, terrified. I had yelled at God, and He yelled back! I still don't know if that voice was audible or not, but it was loud!

Suddenly, I saw my rebellion. I was so ashamed. Then I felt the Lord's love for me. His love flooded the room I was in. I was no longer afraid, just humbled and loved. I was so loved.

Touched by His love, I said, "Yes, Lord. Whatever You want. My life is Yours."

Two years later, I was married to my lovely Chinese wife and living in her hometown: Hong Kong.

That night, God jerked the slack out of me. I needed it. But He loved me even as He raised His voice to get my attention. And love made all the difference. I got up from the floor that night, rebuked, but loved. God didn't use guilt or shame, even though I was being rebellious.

He convicted me. The difference between conviction and condemnation is love.

Jesus' love led Him to the cross where He "forever made perfect" we who are being made Holy. Jesus perfects us. We need to know that so we won't let condemnation keep us from running to God when we fail, when we need Him most.

Activation

Look for the lie. Replace it with the truth.

Satan is a liar. He's very good at it. Is there something in your life that condemns you? Are you weighed down with guilt or shame? Reject the lie and replace it with the truth. Condemnation, guilt, and shame are the tools of the accuser (the devil), not God. God convicts us and loves us into wholeness.

Conviction often sounds something like this, "Dave, I saw what you did. That's not who you are. You are better than that. Come on. Come higher. Let's work on that failing together. I'll help you."

Remind yourself of who you are and what Jesus is doing for you. Declare it.

Jesus set me free from guilt and shame and every aspect of the law and legalism. I will not go back into captivity. I stay free from guilt and shame so I can boldly come to God for myself and others. Boldness enables me to pray prayers that change the world. I am who Jesus says I am. I can do what He says I can do. Jesus' love for me is steadier than my heartbeat; it never changes, no matter what I do. I am free from condemnation, guilt, and shame! Forever!

So Christ has truly set us free. Now make sure that you stay free....

Galatians 5:1 (NLT)

Even if we feel guilty, God is greater than our feelings, and he knows everything. Dear friends, if we don't feel guilty, we can come to God with bold confidence. And we will receive from him whatever we ask because we obey him and do the things that please him.

1 John 3:20-22 (NLT)

III. A Path

Day 5 Jesus Calls, "I am the Way, the Only Way to God."

The Path

In 2017, during a time of worship, I saw a picture in my mind. A moving picture. I'll call it a vision. As I saw things, I began to understand what they meant.

I saw a path. I was walking with Jesus. It was the path of life. Eternal life. I saw the path going down through valleys, around hills and out over the countryside. Far in the distance, it went up to heaven. Somehow, I knew it was my path - the one God prepared for me.

Then I saw a picture of paths going all around the world, into many nations, cities, villages, even reaching isolated places where few people lived. I also saw areas where there were no paths. The path of life goes throughout the earth wherever we go, walking with Jesus. Where we go, people can find the path to God, to life. If we do not go, there is no path for them to find. I thought of missionaries going around the world, creating new paths.

Then, I saw myself back with Jesus, walking the path planned for me. We came to a place in the path where there was a hole. It was a gap in the path shaped like me - an exact fit for my body shape. Suddenly, I realized the path was made up of people, people who laid down their lives to make a way for others to find the way to

God. Many would walk the path. Some would lay down their lives to become the path.

Jesus invited me to lay down my life and become part of the path. I didn't have to think about it. It was what Jesus had prepared for me. I said, "Yes." I laid down and took my place. And people began to walk on me as I had walked on others who made up the path of my life. I saw people who started to wander from the path. And those laid down on the path reached up their hands and gently nudged the wanderers back onto the path.

I wanted to go farther on the path, but I realized it was important for me to fill the gap in the path that was clearly where I fit. I took my place, happy for those who walked on me to go on to do greater things than I ever would.

The Lord has shown me the path many times since then. One morning, I saw the cross. It was open, like a doorway. I walked through the cross and immediately realized I had entered into Jesus who as I came through the cross was carrying a cross – my cross. We walked through His cross and emerged on the path. The path begins at the cross. It is the only entrance to the path.

The visions I saw are a picture of 1 John 3:16.

> This is how we have discovered love's reality: Jesus sacrificed his life for us. Because of this great love, we should be willing to lay down our lives for one another.
> 1 John 3:16 (TPT)

I am so grateful for the many people who touched my life while I was stumbling and bumbling around, trying to live my own life. I didn't appreciate the Christians I met then. I laughed behind their backs and even openly mocked some. But I saw things in their lives that I desperately wanted – no, needed. I found the path to God because of all those who nudged me in the right direction by their words, their examples, and their many acts of kindness. I learned what life could be like with Jesus by watching those people. They didn't know I was watching, but I was.

Living For the Next Generation

Recently, I gained greater perspective on the vision and the meaning of 1 John 3:16.

> Praise the Lord!
> Great blessings belong to those who fear and respect the Lord,
> who are happy to do what he commands.
> **Their descendants will be given**
> **power on earth**.
> Those who do right will be greatly blessed.
> Psalm 112:1-2 (ERV)

The impact of a life (mine and yours) lived for God will flow to the next generation. Our children will be mighty, influential – "given power on earth" because you and I lived wholeheartedly for God. This life isn't just about you or me; it never was.

We lay our lives down, as Jesus did, to become a path for future generations to follow. They will walk on us to go where we did not and do what we could not do.

Most of us will give our lives a few minutes at a time. We will see someone who needs Jesus' love. It will be inconvenient. I can almost guarantee that. And you will have to choose – do what you want, even need to do or interrupt your life to serve theirs. As you listen to the still, small voice inside you, loving others will become a lifestyle. You will become a laid-down lover, a living sacrifice, touching others with the love of Jesus.

> "All God wants is my laid-down love, my reckless devotion. He is asking the same from you."
> --Heidi Baker

Activation

Jesus loves you so much. You are His treasure, and He loves just being with you, walking with you. He has plans for you – great plans. Life with Jesus is this beautiful balance of being with Him, growing to become like Him, and doing things together.

Are you ready for an adventure? Take your place in the path. Declare this over your life:

"I will live my life as a laid-down lover of Jesus Christ. I choose to follow the path Jesus blazed for me. I will take my place in the path of life, the place prepared for me. With great joy, I invest my life in those who will follow. I lay down to be a stepping stone for others to walk on that they may go far and do great things for God. I am thrilled to be part of something so much greater than myself."

Living a Laid-Down Life

> Jesus told him, "I am the way, the truth, and the Life. No one can come to the Father except through Me.
> John 14:6 (NLT)

"I surrender my own life, and no one has the power to take my life from me. I have the authority to lay it down and the power to take it back again. This is the destiny my Father has set before me."

John 10:18 (TPT)

"There is no greater love than to lay down one's life for one's friends."

John 15:13 (NLT)

The first time I laid down my life was in 1988. I surrendered everything. I asked God to give me time with Him. I desperately wanted to walk the path of life He prepared for me. I ended up in China! I should have warned you about that. Too late. You already prayed. Smile. Your adventure has begun.

Day 6 Jesus Calls, "Walk With Me."

> When the cool evening breezes were blowing, the man and his wife heard the Lord God walking about in the garden.
>
> ...Then the Lord God called to the man, "Where are you?"
>
> Genesis 3:8-9 (NLT)

Think about that. God came down to walk with Adam and Eve. The day was cooling down. There was a gentle breeze and God wanted to walk with His children. I don't remember when I first saw this picture, but from that day on I've wanted, more than anything, to walk with God.

But the context of that verse is the worst day in human history. It was the day Adam and Eve died spiritually. And it was the day they gave Satan authority over the whole Earth. (See Day 2 for details)

Enoch Walked With God

After Adam and Eve rejected God and did what Satan suggested, Enoch was the first person to walk with God again. Enoch was my new hero.

Enoch lived during Adam's lifetime. Unlike Adam and Eve, he never lived in the Garden of Eden. Men didn't walk with God the way Adam and Eve had. I wonder if Enoch talked with Adam about what it was like before, in the garden with God.

"Adam, what's God like? What did it feel like when God came down in the evenings and walked with you? What did you talk about? Adam, there's this emptiness inside me. I want to know God. I want to walk with Him."

Enoch somehow got God's attention. Maybe he just wanted to be with God so much that God wanted to be with him. I hoped that was true.

I Want to Walk With You

I walked away from God as a boy. I was 32 when I came back and gave Him my life. I read Genesis 5:24, "Enoch walked faithfully with God; then he was no more, because God took him away," my heart jumped. I wasn't very proud of the way I had lived. I wanted to change almost everything in my life. I longed for God's approval. I came to believe the only way I could make such radical changes in my life was to walk with God.

I explored what happened to Enoch and found:

> It was by faith that Enoch was taken up to heaven without dying— "he disappeared because God took him." For before he was taken up, he was known as a person who pleased God.
> Hebrews 11:5 (NIV)

I had left my wild, alcoholic life, but I had scars — deep, painful wounds. I strived to win God's approval. I wanted to please God. I tried to earn it.

Over the next year, I went to a lot of church services and activities. Some were great, some not so much. But none of them came anywhere close to walking with God. I grew in desperation to be with God, to KNOW Him, to please Him. I had a few experiences with Jesus.

They made me hungry for more. I didn't want to stop short of actually walking with Him.

I studied the Bible. I was thrilled to find that God wants to walk together:

> "And I will walk among you and will be your God, and you will be my people.
> Leviticus 26:12 (NIV)
> "...and what does the Lord require of you but to do justice, to love kindness, and to walk humbly with your God?
> Micah 6:8 (NASB)

Maybe the evening walks in the Garden of Eden were God's idea. I clung to that thought.

Anyone who has read the Bible knows that only a handful of people ever walked closely with God in the Old Testament. The history of Israel's kings is a chariot wreck of immorality and ungodliness. Even the heroes of faith who walked close to God for a season had horrible moments in their lives. It was discouraging to see how badly people failed God in the Old Testament. How could I do better than them?

In the New Testament, I saw Jesus walking with His disciples. I envied the disciples, but I thought Enoch's experience was even greater because it was one-on-one. That's what I wanted.

And that's what I found.

One on One With Jesus

It took a long time and a lot of wrong ideas before I realized that Jesus came to reunite us with God. To make sure we stay heart-connected to God, the Holy Spirit comes to live in us. From the moment we are "born again" we have the Holy Spirit in us.

> Since we live by the Spirit, let us keep in step with the Spirit.
> Galatians 5:25 (NIV)

Men struggled so much walking with God, that He put His Spirit in us so we can keep in step with Him. Awesome! Like Enoch, we can walk with God. Jesus made it possible.

> Then Jesus said, "Come to me, all of you who are weary and carry heavy burdens, and I will give you rest. Take my yoke upon you. Let me teach you, because I am humble and gentle at heart, and you will find rest for your souls. For my yoke is easy to bear, and the burden I give you is light."
> Matthew 11:28-30 (NLT)

Jesus invited us to be yoked with Him. When I was a boy, I loved to watch our Amish farmer neighbors plowing fields with a team of horses and a plow they walked behind. Every spring I would watch as the plow carved straight furrows, revealing rich, black Pennsylvania soil. Furrow after furrow in long fields, uphill and down, hour after hour. The horses had to be exactly in step to pull the plow. That's what Jesus is talking about in His invitation. Being yoked to Jesus means walking with Him, side by side, step by step, when life is easy and when life is hard. Inseparable.

I reread Matthew 11:28-30 and saw a picture of Jesus, and I yoked together, a team, walking side by side. If I could learn how to live like that, walking side by side with Jesus, I knew I could become who the Bible says I am and do amazing things for God. Yoked to Jesus, I could.

I've always been a radical. When I was a sinner, I was good at it. I was wild. I drank so much that I finally had to face the fact I was an alcoholic. I was a happy drunk, so no one seemed to mind. But, deep inside, I was dying. I hated myself and my life more every day. I tried to stop. Again, and again. I couldn't.

I went to AA. It helped. But I sat beside guys in AA who would disappear for months, then come in one night stinking and drunk. I was so afraid I would become one of them. The craving I had for alcohol was all-consuming.

After six months of shaky sobriety, I gave my life to Jesus. I began praying, "Jesus, if I could just be with you, I know I would never go back to my old life. Let me work for you full time, so I will never go back to my alcoholic life." I prayed fervently. I began looking for Christian jobs. But who would want an alcoholic lawyer who had been sober for less than a year?

Jesus did.

One day I got a phone call asking if I wanted to go to China for a year teaching law and business with a Christian organization. I asked a lot of questions. I prayed. It meant leaving my townhouse-on-a-golf-course, lawyer life and moving far away from everything and everyone I knew. The pay was ridiculous, the conditions harsh. I said "Yes."

Teaching in China was as hard as they said it would be. I was alone a lot. My school was isolated. No car. I had a bicycle. Television was crop reports and communist propaganda, all in Chinese, of course. I had limited phone access. It took two weeks to send a letter, another two to receive an answer. Everyday life was harder; China was still a third world nation in 1989. My language ability was limited. And I loved it!

I spent more time with Jesus than I thought possible. I had to rely on Him to deal with the daily struggles I faced. I began to hear His voice. He answered my prayers in amazing ways. The Bible came alive and spoke to me. He comforted me when times got tough. I felt Jesus' love for the Chinese people. I learned to walk with Jesus, not only for myself but for others. What joy! I felt more alive than I had in a long, long time.

My walk with Jesus began with a big step – a big surrender. I gave up everything I had: friends, familiar culture, my career, and a very comfortable lifestyle. That was a big step. But I needed to take a big step to break free from my old life of addiction and pain. You may not need to make such a drastic step. Just take a step, one step toward Jesus. And He will meet you and walk with you.

Activation

Pray this short prayer. *Jesus, I want to walk with You. Wherever You want to go, that's where we will go. Whatever you want to do, that's what we'll do. I want to hear Your voice. I want to know Your heart. I want to walk with You.*

Now, take daily steps toward walking with Jesus. Meet Jesus tomorrow morning, the next, and the next... You're going to have a great life!

IV. A Process: Be With Jesus, Become Like Jesus, and Do Things With Jesus

A. Be With Jesus

Day 7 Jesus Calls, "I am Your Daily Bread."

August 12, 2017 Journal

I needed to be reassured of Jesus' love for me. I was in physical pain, and it was blinding me – all I could see was the pain. So, I asked, "Jesus, how are You loving me right now in ways I can't see?"

He said, "You've been drinking from the wrong pool. You've been drinking from the pool of dark thoughts, the pools of discouragement and despair. You think you are in a desert. You think there is a dark cloud over you. Look up. It is a rain cloud!!"

Jesus laughed. "Drink only the water I give. Sweet water of life. Not the bitter waters of human life, but the water from the heavens. **Open your mouth and I will fill it.** As the ravens fed Elijah, I will feed you. Spiritual drink, spiritual food. I will sustain you. «

"Now get up, dust yourself off and get going. You're walking with me."

> **"Open wide your mouth and I will fill it."**
> Psalm 81:10 (NIV)

Since then, Jesus has reminded me of this wonderful promise again and again. Every morning I come to Him, open to be filled with what He has for me that day. He always comes. He often gives me things I won't know I need until much later.

Manna from Heaven

The Israelites were finally free from slavery in Egypt. God had done amazing miracles to get them this far. But now they were in a desert. There was no food, no water. The people complained.

> Then the Lord said to Moses, "I will rain down bread from heaven for you. **The people are to go out each day and gather enough for that day. In this way, I will test them and see whether they will follow my instructions.**"
>
> ...and in the morning there was a layer of dew around the camp. When the dew was gone, thin flakes like frost on the ground appeared on the desert floor. When the Israelites saw it, they said to each other, "What is it?" For they did not know what it was.
>
> Moses said to them, "It is the bread the Lord has given you to eat. This is what the Lord has commanded: 'Everyone is to gather as much as they need. Take an omer for each person you have in your tent.'"
>
> The Israelites did as they were told; some gathered much, some little. And when they measured it by the omer, the one who gathered much did not have too much, and the one who gathered little did not have too little. Everyone had gathered just as much as they needed.
>
> Then Moses said to them, "No one is to keep any of it until morning."

However, some of them paid no attention to Moses; they kept part of it until morning, but it was full of maggots and began to smell. So, Moses was angry with them.

Each morning everyone gathered as much as they needed, and when the sun grew hot, it melted away.

The people of Israel called the bread manna. It was white like coriander seed and tasted like wafers made with honey.

Exodus 16:4, 13-21, 31 (NIV)

For 40 years, the bread of God fell from heaven six days a week (the manna for the 7th day of rest was collected on the sixth day). The manna had to be gathered first thing in the morning. Once the sun grew hot, the manna melted and was gone. Each day's manna was only for that day. By the next morning, it would be rotten and have maggots. No matter how much people gathered, a little or a lot, when measured, it was enough (1 omer per person is 2.3 quarts or 2.2 liters).

The physical nourishment of the whole nation of Israel had to be painstakingly picked off the desert floor – little flakes lying in the sand. It would take a lot of manna flakes to make 2.3 quarts. If you were late, it was gone, melted by the sun. You couldn't hoard it. Overnight, it rotted and became full of maggots. Manna was life to them. Either you developed a daily routine of gathering your manna or you starved.

God made it clear why He provided for them in this way. It was a test of obedience. And it was to make the people rely on Him every day. God provided, but people had to gather what He gave them every morning.

It is the same with us today. God has bread from heaven for us. We need to gather it first thing every morning. Yesterday's bread won't be good today. We need fresh bread.

If I don't meet with Jesus first thing in the morning, the day has a way of taking over. Appointments, work, phone calls, and distractions fill my heart and my mind. I am no longer available mentally or emotionally even if I can grab a few minutes to "be with Jesus."

"I will be Your Daily Bread."

> "The truth is," Jesus said, "Moses didn't give you the bread of heaven. It's my Father who offers bread that comes as a dramatic sign from heaven. The bread of God is the One who came out of heaven to give his life to feed the world."
>
> "Then please, sir, give us this bread every day," they replied.
>
> Jesus said to them, "**I am the Bread of Life. Come every day to me and you will never be hungry. Believe in me and you will never be thirsty.**"
>
> John 6:32-35 (TPT)

The physical bread of God for the Israelites was manna. Today, we have much better bread. Jesus is the Bread of Life that falls fresh into our lives every day. "The bread that comes down from heaven and gives life to the world." Jesus doesn't just give us bread every day. He offers us Himself.

The test of our discipleship is whether we will receive Jesus and walk with Him today or will we stumble and bumble through the day on our own? Jesus is saying,

"Obey Me and I will be able to be there for you. I'll help you. I want to do so much for you. Come to Me. Stay with Me."

> Jesus replied, "All who love me will do what I say. My Father will love them, and we will come and make our home with each of them."
> John 14:23 (NLT)

Activation

The one thing that has changed my walk with Jesus more than any other is the commitment to begin every day with Jesus. The rare days when I get drawn away from Him before my day actually begins rarely go well. Take the plunge. Make the commitment to meet Him every morning. Tell Him:

Every morning I will meet with You, Jesus, to collect what You have for me that day. Your provision rains down upon me. You know what is going to happen to me today and every day. You know what I need to be protected, energized, whole and well. In my morning delight time, You give me everything I need for each day. You give me your love, joy, peace, patience... everything I will need to be like You that day. You also give me anointing, provision, warnings, words of encouragement, wisdom, and direction for myself and for others. All of this is topped with the joy of just being with You and knowing You will walk with me each day.

Set a time and a place for just you and Jesus. Make an appointment to meet with Jesus tomorrow and keep your appointment. You just passed the manna test.

Day 8 Jesus Calls, "Meet Me in My Word."

> "The Bible is alive, it speaks to me; it has feet, it runs after me; it has hands, it lays hold of me."
> - Martin Luther

October 11, 2018, I was having my Delight/Desire time with Jesus as I began my day.

For weeks, I have felt change in the air. I don't know what God is going to do, but I feel a change is coming. I had that feeling again as I read *Knowing Your Purpose* in Arthur Burk's devotional: *Blessing Your Spirit*.

I was listening to praise and worship from Bethel Church in Redding as I opened my Bible. I felt the Lord prompt me to look at Hebrews.

The worship finished and one of Bethel's leaders, Paul Manwaring, began to speak, "They had been wandering for 40 years. Their leader was dead. The promised land was the other side of the Jordan. Joshua said, 'Consecrate yourselves. Set yourselves apart and see what great wonders the Lord will do among you."[6]

I looked down as my Bible opened to Hebrews. This scripture was highlighted: "They grieved God for forty years by sinning in their unbelief until they dropped dead in the desert." Hebrews 3:17 (TPT)

Whoa! Jesus, you have my attention.

I looked up the scripture Paul was talking about: "Consecrate yourselves. Set yourselves apart and see

---

[6] https://www.youtube.com/watch?v=oW-pHVPAATs&t=542s at the 24 minute mark.

what great wonders the Lord will do among you," is a paraphrase of Joshua 3:5.

Jesus, what does this mean – for me? Jesus showed me a picture. In that picture, I was a stake, driven into the ground of a nation I love. He was telling me to prepare to go to that country.

What should I do? I reread Joshua 3:5. Consecrate yourself. Sanctify yourself. Prepare to see what great things God is going to do. I looked up consecrate and sanctify.

Jesus was telling me to get ready. As the time for this trip approaches, He will reveal more. I noticed the focus of the preparation was myself – my heart. I am still preparing for that trip.

This is one of the hundreds of times the Lord has spoken to me through scripture.

The Bible is the Holy Spirit Speaking to You

The same Holy Spirit who hovered over the earth creating as God spoke, the One who baptized Jesus with Himself and with power, the One who raised Jesus from the dead, the Holy Spirit who will lead you and guide you into all truth and will show you what is to come - He is the one who inspired the writers of each book of the Bible. That Holy Spirit breathed life into the Scripture.

> Every Scripture has been written by the Holy Spirit, the breath of God. It will empower you by its instruction and correction, giving you the strength to take the right direction and lead you deeper into the path of godliness.
> 2 Timothy 3:16 (TPT)

The author of Hebrews writes "as the Holy Spirit says" then quotes Psalm 95.

> So, **as the Holy Spirit says**: "Today, if you hear his voice, do not harden your hearts...."
> Hebrews 3:7 (NIV)

The author of Hebrews is saying **the Bible is the Holy Spirit speaking**.

So, don't be surprised to hear God, Jesus or the Holy Spirit as you read the Bible. At times, I hear God, sometimes the Holy Spirit, but I'm fascinated with Jesus. Maybe that's why I have most of my experiences with Him. They are all God. And when you read the Bible with a listening heart, you WILL hear God.

Meet Jesus in His Word

If you are a Christian, you hear Jesus. Jesus said it. It's true.

> "But the one who enters through the gate is the shepherd of the sheep. The gatekeeper opens the gate for him, and the sheep recognize his voice and come to him. He calls his own sheep by name and leads them out. After he has gathered his own flock, he walks ahead of them, and they follow him because they know his voice. They won't follow a stranger; they will run from him because they don't know his voice."
> "I have other sheep, too, that are not in this sheepfold. I must bring them also. They will listen to my voice, and there will be one flock with one shepherd.

> My sheep listen to my voice; I know them, and
> they follow me.
> John 10:2-5, 16, 27 (NLT)

Believer, you are Jesus' sheep. He called your name! You
are a Christian today because you heard His voice and
followed Him. Keep listening. He's still speaking.

Everything changes when you come to the Bible expecting to meet Jesus.

The life of God is in this fantastic book. Come to the
Bible expecting to encounter Him and you will. A lot of
seasoned Christians will tell you that God most often
speaks to them through His Word.

I used to read the Bible only with my mind. That's kind
of silly because the Bible says the things of God are
foolishness to the human mind.

> The person without the Spirit does not accept
> the things that come from the Spirit of God
> but considers them foolishness, and cannot
> understand them because they are discerned
> only through the Spirit.
> 1 Corinthians 2:14 (NIV)

When I read with my heart and my mind, I'm reading to
be touched, to be changed. I read to encounter Jesus.
I read to receive God's truth, to allow that truth to go
deep into the soil of my heart. I invite Jesus to change
me as I read. I pour out my heart and invite Him to fill it.

Plant the Living Seed of God's Word

That Bible sitting on your shelf is filled with seeds of
realities that God wants to happen.

What most of us can't wrap our minds around is that when we open our Bible and read, we are having an encounter with God. Reading these God-breathed words is God planting the living Word seeds in our hearts. And as we unite God's word with our willing hearts and our faith in God and His goodness, the seeds become realities in our lives and in our world.

> For through the eternal and living Word of God you have been born again. And this "seed" that he planted within you can never be destroyed but will live *and grow* inside of you forever.
> 1 Peter 1:23 (TPT)

As you read the Bible, it reads you. "It exposes your innermost thoughts and desires."

> For the word of God is alive and powerful. It is sharper than the sharpest two-edged sword, cutting between soul and spirit, between joint and marrow. **It exposes our innermost thoughts and desires.** Nothing in all creation is hidden from God. Everything is naked and exposed before his eyes, and he is the one to whom we are accountable.
> Hebrews 4:12-13 (NLT)

Reinhard Bonnke said it this way, "The Bible is a book you can completely rely on to tell you the truth about God – and about yourself."

Reading God's Word plants the life of God in your heart. When you read wanting and expecting it to change you, your faith calls the seeds to life, and you are changed.

This is the only Living Book in the world. To read the Bible is to hear the Holy Spirit speak. As you read you will find specific words that are answers to your immediate problems and questions. The Holy Spirit will highlight them. They will "jump out" at you. You will meet Jesus there. He will comfort you. He will calm your fears. He will encourage you. He will bring you joy. He will give you strength, wisdom, and courage to do what you need to do. And you will be changed.

Plant Living Word Seeds in People, in Nations

When we pray God's Word, we release the life in His Word seeds into the person, the situation or the nation we are praying for. God seeded space with Word seeds and planets appeared. He created everything by Word seeds, boldly declared. The world we live in is the result of God's words spoken with the intent to create and change what was into what is. Jesus sustains everything "[the entire physical and spiritual universe] by His powerful word" Hebrews 1:3 (AMP).

We, like God and Jesus, can "speak life" as we release God's Word into the lost and dying world around us. It begins when we meet Jesus in God's Word.

Activation

Two Questions to Guide You as The Bible Speaks to You

In Acts 2, we see 120 people praying in an upper room, waiting for the power Jesus promised to fall on them. It was during the Jewish feast of Pentecost and Jerusalem was filled with Jews from all over the world. Then it happened. The 120 were baptized in the Holy Spirit, and it was amazing. The Jewish people saw the 120 when they came down from that experience. It was apparent they were local people, but they were creating a scene because they praised God in languages from all over the world.

> And we all hear these people speaking in our own languages about the wonderful things God has done!" They stood there amazed and perplexed. **"What can this mean?"** they asked each other.
>
> (Acts 2:11-12 (NLT)

Peter stood up and spoke to the crowd. He told them about Jesus.

> Peter's words pierced their hearts, and they said to him and to the other apostles, "Brothers, **what should we do**?"
>
> Acts 2:37 (NLT)

When God speaks or does something new or something we don't understand, we should ask:

1. **What does this mean?**

Unless the Holy Spirit reveals spiritual things to you, you won't understand. No one can. So, ask. "What does this mean, Lord?"

> But the person who is not a Christian does not understand these words from the Holy Spirit. He thinks they are foolish. He cannot understand them because he does not have the Holy Spirit to help him understand.
>
> 1 Corinthians 2:14 (NLV)

2. **What should I do?**

A willing heart is the key to opening the secrets and deep truths of God's Word.

> Jesus answered them by saying, "My teaching is not My own, but His who sent Me. **If anyone is willing to do His will, he will know** whether the teaching is of God or whether I speak on My own accord *and* by My own authority.
> John 7:16-17 (AMP)

If you are willing, Jesus will not just tell you, He will show you and walk with you. And that's His deepest desire in reaching out to us - to have our hearts desire one thing: Him.

Read your Bible today expecting Jesus to speak to you. Be curious. Ask Him, "What does this mean?" and "What should I do?" Ask, be willing to do what He shows you and He will answer.

Isaiah prophesied about a time when God, Himself would teach His people. Jesus brought this time to pass. "All your children shall be taught by the Lord...." Isaiah 54:13 (NKJV)

Day 9 Jesus calls, "Delight in Me, I Will Give You the Desires of Your Heart."

> "How I love your law! I think about it
> all day long."
> Psalm 119:97 (GNT)

I reread the verse. It wasn't true. For me. Of course, it was true for David, but I didn't "love" scripture. I studied scripture. I had "devotions" every day. I read the Bible. I tried to understand it. I taught it. I prayed it. I believed it. But I didn't delight in it. I didn't love scripture the way David did.

What was I missing? There had to be more. I was trained as a lawyer, but I didn't want to approach God's Word like a Pharisee. But I did. In my mind, I was looking for answers. I wanted to know the rules. What's right? What's wrong? How can I do that?

The Psalms read more like love letters than rules. I can't fully describe what was happening in me at that moment when I realized I didn't love the Bible the way David did. Let me just say, "I grieved." I wanted a relationship with Jesus, but I was chained to legalism. After all, I was a lawyer. That's how I saw the world, and that's how I saw God's Word.

My intellectual approach to God wasn't satisfying. I hungered to know and love Jesus, to linger on God's words the way I lingered on every word Karen said. Karen was my friend – okay, she was more than a friend. I was struggling to admit how much I was in love with her. Karen and I were a world apart. I was in Pennsylvania; she was in Hong Kong. We talked by phone. The calls were short because five minutes cost more than a good dinner out. I treasured every word she said, the lilt of her voice, her quirky grammar and mashed up phrasing (English is Karen's fourth language), her wit, and wisdom. I replayed those calls in my mind hours, even days later. My heart soared. I loved, I truly loved her words.

I went on a journey to love the Bible the way David did. I began reading the Psalms every morning. One morning, I read Psalm 37:4 (NASB): Delight yourself in the Lord; And He will give you the desires of your heart.

"Delight yourself in the Lord, and He will give you the desires of your heart," came alive to me. It was a promise. I pursued the promise.

I slowly read through the Psalms every morning until I found a verse that caught my attention. Some mornings my heart jumped with joy. "Wow! That's so cool." I found them – dozens of verses that touched me on an emotional level. I stopped each morning after I found one of those verses.

I wrote down what I felt, what I loved about that verse. Then I responded to that verse. From delight, what desires arose? At first, I was still very much in Bible study mode, but over weeks I began to have days when I just enjoyed meeting Jesus in the Psalms. And He spoke to me. It was like a conversation. It wasn't just looking for knowledge. I was connecting with the heart behind those verses.

Some mornings, I felt like the string of a cello; the Psalm vibrated, it resonated somewhere deep inside me. It was alive. The words came to life in me. And I began to love meeting Jesus there. I wrote down my experiences. I treasured what He revealed and spoke to me. I marveled at the peace and joy I felt. I loved those precious times when Jesus opened His Word to me. Even more, I loved the experiences we were having together. And my desire for Jesus grew. I began to act on my desires. Jesus filled them as I pursued Him.

At first, I didn't write everything in my journal, and I lost some things Jesus told me. Those insights were precious to me. I didn't believe I would forget them so easily, but I did. So, I began to journal every morning. For years I have been faithful in keeping my delight/desire journal. I love to read back and see how Jesus met me and how I have been changed by delighting in His Word.

Nothing I have ever done has impacted my life more than taking delight in scripture and acting on it. Delight becomes desire and desire becomes a pursuit. Pursuing Jesus is fun because He wants to be found. It's like when I played hide and seek with my nieces and nephews when they were small. I hid but in obvious places. I wanted them to find me. Jesus wants us to pursue Him and find Him.

Today, open your Bible expecting to meet Jesus there. Give Him time, and you will experience the joy of meeting with Him daily. Reading the Bible won't be a discipline that you enforce with your willpower; it will become a delight. From that delight of meeting Jesus in His Word, desires will be birthed in your heart - needs that must be filled. Heart desires.

Activation

The key to meeting Jesus in scripture is responding to the Bible with your heart, not just your mind. Why not meet Jesus today in a Delight/Desire experience?

This should take ten to fifteen minutes at most.

1. Turn to a new page in your journal or open a document or note. Write these headings:

Today's Date:

Delight:

Desire:

2. Slowly read Psalm 23 in a translation you usually don't read. I've found this is a great way to have scripture become fresh and new. (I recommend The Passion Translation or New Living Translation. You will find them on BibleGateway.com.)

Read until you see something that makes your heart jump – a strong, positive, emotional response to a word, phrase or verse.

(**Make it personal.** Read the scripture with your name in it or see yourself receiving or doing what the scripture says. **I sometimes read aloud.** Hearing the words helps me discover things I haven't seen before.)

3. Write down what you "delight" about that word, phrase or verse. Just write what you feel and what that means to you.

Delight:

4. What desire does that word, phrase or verse trigger in you? Think about it. Write it down. Follow it. What about that do you want in your life?

Desire:

Scripture makes us hungry for more of Jesus. Respond with your heart – your desires. All actions begin with desires. All change begins with a change of heart. This is how Jesus reaches us. This is how He changes us. We change what we do when we change what we want.

Is your desire strong enough to make you want to take an action step? Not every desire is for immediate action. But some are. Expect to do something about your new-found desires. If this desire makes you want to do so something, think about what **simple step** you can take **right now** to begin to **pursue that desire**. Do it.

Here's My Delight/Desire Journal Entry

I read Psalm 23 in The Passion Translation.

> *The Lord is my best friend and my shepherd.*
> Psalm 23:1 (TPT)

Delight: "Best friend?" What an amazing thought. I love that! But where did that translation come from? I read the translator's note. The Hebrew word for Shepherd is *ra'ah*, which is also the Hebrew word for "best friend." That makes me feel so much closer to Jesus than shepherd. I understand the metaphor, but knowing He is both shepherd and best friend makes me think. Jesus treats me like a friend.

Desire: I want that!! I want to live with Jesus as my "best friend." I'm stumbling a little over that idea. I'm not there yet, but I want to be. We say Jesus is our friend, but to really live that way…. Best friend. I reread verse 1. While my mind still struggles with the idea, I have a fresh realization that is what Jesus wants.

Action Step: January 10, 2019. I didn't have an action step when I had this experience. Now, as I'm editing the final draft of this book, I realize Jesus is waiting. He wants me to pursue our friendship at a new level. Because my mind is still struggling, I asked Him, "Jesus, how are You being a best friend to me?"

Crickets. I didn't hear anything. I am in pain again in my spine. Fogged in. How embarrassing is this? I'm trying to show you something, and I failed. It's time to be real. There are times I don't hear well. Pain – emotional and physical, makes it hard to hear Jesus. But that doesn't mean He isn't speaking. I've heard Him too many times to doubt Him now. I wrote "Jesus, how are You being a best friend to me?" in my journal for tomorrow morning and went to rest.

January 11, 2019. Good morning, Jesus. I have to admit, I struggled with the idea of You being my best friend. But that's what Psalm 23 says. So, I'm asking, "Jesus, how are You being a best friend to me?"

My first impression was me thinking of pain and how I got stuck in it yesterday. I saw a mental picture of pain as a fog that grew and covered me. I saw a thick layer of fog covering my part of the world; it was everywhere I went. I saw Jesus reaching down from heaven, His arm reaching through the fog. He offered me His hand. I took it. He pulled me up above the pain and sat me above the fog of pain.

Jesus, I know that was from You. Give me a scripture to stand on, above the pain. I felt Jesus was saying to open my Bible to where I left off yesterday. I had been reading Psalm 25 in the Passion Translation. I thought, *I don't think there are any healing scriptures in Psalm 25.*

What if I fail again? Doubt was knocking at my door. I'm not opening that door.

This is what I saw when I opened my Kindle. The first full sentence at the top of the page says:

> **Rescue me, Lord, for you're my only Hero**.
> Psalm 25:15 (TPT)

Wow! I'm sitting here with a big smile on my face, quietly laughing. I remember Jesus' hand reaching through the fog of pain to pull me above it and sit me on top of the pain. *"Rescue me, Lord, for you're my Only Hero."*

You never cease to amaze me, Jesus! This is why I pursue you. One word from You changes everything! I read on. What amazing promises to stand on:

> ...Come closer to me now, Lord, for I need your mercy.
> ...Can't you feel my pain?
> ...Let it never be said that I trusted You and You didn't come to my rescue.
> Psalm 25:16, 18, 20 (TPT)

Now, if you haven't already, do this activation for yourself.

Day 10 Jesus Calls, "Meet Me in Praise."

> Then Moses said to him, "**If your Presence does
> not go with us**, do not send us up from here.
> How will anyone know that you are pleased
> with me and with your people unless you go
> with us? **What else will distinguish me and
> your people from all the other people on the
> face of the earth**?"
> And the Lord said to Moses, "I will do the very
> thing you have asked because I am pleased with
> you and I know you by name."
> Exodus 33:15-17 (NIV)

God was frustrated with the Israelites. They were
stubborn, disobedient and rebellious. God said he
would send an angel with them on their journey to the
Promised Land, but God would not go with them. Moses
refused to go on without God's presence. Moses asked
two questions that you and I need to ask:

> How will anyone know that you are pleased with
> me and with your people unless you go with us?
> What else will distinguish me and your
> people from all the other people on the face
> of the earth?

We need God's presence. In His presence we experience
God, and we are forever changed. It is God's presence in
and on our lives that others see. That's what they want.

We Meet God in Praise and Worship

> Enter his gates with thanksgiving; go into his
> courts with praise. Give thanks to him and
> praise his name.

Psalm 100:4 (NLT)

You ·sit as the Holy One [L are holy]. The praises
of Israel are your throne [L You are enthroned
on the praises of Israel].

Psalm 22:3 (EXB)

Jack Hayford explains Psalm 22:3 this way, "Wherever
God's people come together to worship, we become a
habitation for His presence. God comes to dwell where
His people worship...."[7]

When God shows up, He changes everything.

When God shows up (His tangible presence) changes
everything. Some of the greatest changes in my life
happened while worshiping. Fears, anger, and doubts
that were clinging to me fell away in the presence of
the Living God. Sometimes I knew what God was doing.
Sometimes I didn't. But the changes He made were real
and lasting.

Submit yourselves, then, to God. Resist the
devil, and he will flee from you. Come near to
God and he will come near to you.

James 4:7-8 (NIV)

What would that look like?

I lived in Hong Kong for twelve years. Most of the 7.5
million people in Hong Kong practice Chinese folk
religion: a combination of Buddhism, Daoism, ancestral
worship and worshiping local gods. There are altars
in most businesses; street shrines and neighborhood
temples are everywhere. Most apartments have

---

[7] https://www.jackhayford.org/teaching/articles/
why-and-how-we-worship/

altars where sacrifices are made, and incense is burned. In fact, Hong Kong means "fragrant harbor." It was named after the fragrance of incense burning throughout the island.

For the 850,000 Christians in Hong Kong, this creates some challenges. Without realizing it, our friends and neighbors are worshipping demons. Often, we would go into a restaurant or a home where someone genuinely worshipped these "gods" or "ancestors," and there would be a dark presence there. Let me give specific examples.

My wife's parents were wonderful, Christian people. When Daddy passed away, we went to the funeral home for his funeral. The funeral home was huge. Many services were going on at the same time. Mostly Buddhist. We could hear the wailing of people who had lost loved ones. People were burning paper "money," "cars" and other images of things they thought their loved one would need in the afterlife. Incense, smoke, and fear filled the air. The anguished cries of despair were heart-rending. It was a dark, dark place. I was shocked at the intensity of the dark presences I felt there.

We went early to prepare the room for the funeral. We had invited friends from our praise and worship team to come and clear the atmosphere. We walked around the room, praising Jesus, inviting God to fill the atmosphere with His glory. We began to worship with all our hearts. You could literally feel the darkness being pushed back. The sweet presence of the Lord, the presence of life and hope filled the room. The team continued praising and worshiping throughout the time we were there. People who attended the funeral noticed the difference.

They talked about it. And we had several hope-filled conversations with unbelievers about Jesus that day. Light drives out darkness. God inhabits the praises of His people.

Another time, we were in Victoria Park on Hong Kong Island, doing a praise and worship event using the harp and bowl model of praise and declaration. Some local Buddhists were having their regular Tai Chi exercises in that part of the park. They came over and complained that we were disturbing their Chi (loosely translated as "spiritual energy") and ruining their experience. Hmmm.

One last example. Every time someone in our church moved into a new apartment, we had to do a house cleansing. When people have altars to demons and actively sacrifice to them, territorial spirits will come into these homes. A couple in the home fellowship we led told us they couldn't sleep at night. They would hear strange sounds in the kitchen – pots and pans clanging, etc. It was more than a little scary.

We went to their home. I immediately sensed a dark presence there. I didn't have a clue what to do. I asked Jesus, "What do You want us to do?" He said, "Just praise Me." We walked around the apartment, praising Jesus in each room. By the time we got to the bedrooms, we were rejoicing, praising and worshiping God. We heard a loud noise in the kitchen, and then we all sensed a breakthrough. The spirit was gone. It never came back. The good news is that the greatest territorial spirit is the Holy Spirit. He inhabits the praises of His people.

Praise and worship bring God's presence into your problems.

> In worship, God imparts Himself to us.
> - C.S. Lewis

The examples above were group praise and worship. But the same thing happens when you and I are alone, just us and Jesus. I've had times when I'm struggling with physical pain, depression, rejection – so many things, and the last thing I felt like doing was praising or worshiping God.

I put on the most anointed worship music I can find. I enter His gates with thanksgiving. And I come into His courts with praise. I boldly approach the throne of grace and mercy to find help in my time of need. Praise changes atmospheres. But most of all, praise changes me. I have never left God's presence without being uplifted. Never.

And from that higher place, I fight my battles. Problems look so different when God raises you above them. Sometimes praise and worship are the battle. After praise and worship, what you wanted to pray for is already done. I've seen many people healed while praising God. That's not surprising. God sent Israel's praise and worship team ahead of the army in 2 Chronicles 20:20-26. He still does.

Praise is a Weapon

> God's high and holy praises fill their mouths, for their shouted praises are their weapons of war!
> Psalm 149:6 (TPT)

As you open your mouth and praise God, you are releasing weapons of war into your circumstances. I know that sounds wild, but God showed us how praise wins battles here on earth. Jehoshaphat, king of Israel, received word that a vast army was coming. They were dangerously near. He asked God what to do. All the people fasted and prayed. God spoke to the king through a prophet. And then this happened:

> After consulting the people, Jehoshaphat appointed men to sing to the Lord and to praise him for the splendor of his holiness as they went out at the head of the army, saying:
>
> "Give thanks to the Lord, for his love endures forever."
>
> As they began to sing and praise, the Lord set ambushes against the men of Ammon and Moab and Mount Seir who were invading Judah, and they were defeated. The Ammonites and Moabites rose up against the men from Mount Seir to destroy and annihilate them. After they finished slaughtering the men from Seir, they helped to destroy one another.
>
> When the men of Judah came to the place that overlooks the desert and looked toward the vast army, they saw only dead bodies lying on the ground; no one had escaped.

2 Chronicles 20:21-24 (NIV)

How amazing is that? I have seen miracles happen when people praised God. You will too! Praise invites Jesus into our problems. His presence is greater than our problems.

Activation

Are you struggling with something? Meet Jesus in thanksgiving, praise, and worship. You won't feel like it. In fact, it will probably be the last thing you want to do. Do it anyway!

I create playlists of anointed praise and worship which carries me into God's presence. I prepare for the tough times that will come. The anointed praise and worship really help on days when I'm struggling. Praise and worship your way into God's presence and let Jesus lead you to overcome whatever you are facing.

Day 11 Jesus Calls, "Come, Let Me Teach You My Ways."

Overcoming Opposition to Make God's Dream Come True

Joseph was the eleventh of Jacob's twelve sons and his father's favorite. Joseph's ten older half-brothers hated him because their father loved him more than them. When he was 17, Joseph had two dreams. In the dreams, his brothers and father bowed before him. Joseph told his brothers and his father his dreams. Joseph's older half-brothers were outraged.

When Joseph came to them in the fields, far from their father, they planned to kill him. But the oldest brother convinced them to sell Joseph to a camel caravan of spice merchants going to Egypt. The brothers ripped Joseph's robe, dipped it in blood, and told their father a wild beast had killed him. Jacob grieved.

Joseph was sold as a slave in Egypt. He worked wholeheartedly for Potiphar, his master. God blessed everything Joseph did. Potiphar noticed and made Joseph head of his household. Potiphar's wife tried to seduce Joseph – repeatedly. He refused. Furious because Joseph rejected her advances, she tore her clothes and accused Joseph of trying to rape her.

After eleven years of faithful service, Joseph was wrongly imprisoned. At that point in his life, it would have been easy for Joseph to believe God didn't care about him at all. He went from favorite son to slave, cut off from his mother, father, and younger brother whom he loved. He worked hard and became head of Potiphar's household, but he was still a slave. Finally, he went to prison for a crime he didn't do. In fact, he was in prison because he did the right thing. How dark the nights must have been in the squalor of that Egyptian prison for young Joseph.

Joseph was in prison for over two years. I wonder how many times he asked, "God, where are you?" Does anything hurt more than being punished for something you didn't do? But Joseph was steadfast. He worked diligently and was put in charge of all the inmates. There is no written record of what Joseph went through in those dark years. But we can be sure of this: God was with him. After God gives us a dream for our lives, we can expect opposition. And we can expect God to be there with us, in the prison of our adversity.

Finally, Joseph interpreted a dream for Pharaoh. God revealed there would be a great famine. Joseph proposed a plan to prepare Egypt for the famine. Pharaoh believed Joseph and was impressed with the wisdom of his plan. Pharaoh made Joseph overseer of all of Egypt. Joseph prepared Egypt for the famine.

During the famine, Joseph's older brothers came to Egypt for grain. No one else had any. Finally, Joseph's family joined him in Egypt – over twenty-three years after his brothers betrayed him and sold him into slavery. God's people were saved from a deadly famine by Joseph. Joseph's dreams came true, but only after his character grew.

(See Joseph's story in Genesis 37-47.)

The Lord Tested and Refined Joseph's Character

> But he had already sent a man ahead of his people to Egypt; it was Joseph, who was sold as a slave. His feet were bruised by strong shackles, and his soul was held by iron. *God's promise to Joseph purged his character until it was time for his dreams to come true.*
>
> Psalm 105:17-19 (TPT)
>
> *Until the time came to fulfill his dreams, the LORD tested Joseph's character.*
>
> Psalm 105:19 (NLT)
>
> Until the time that his word [of prophecy regarding his brothers] came true, *the word of the Lord tested and refined him.*
>
> Psalm 105:19 (AMP)

Joseph was God's provision for Israel. Joseph would save his people. But Joseph, the spoiled, favorite son of an overindulgent father wasn't much use to God. He didn't have the character yet to become the man God needed him to be.

God was teaching Joseph some of the hardest lessons of love:

> "Love is patient...." 1 Corinthians 13:4 (NLT).

Twenty-three years after Joseph's dreams of his family bowing to him, they did. And he saved them. The 17-year-old was now 40. Think about eleven years of slavery, two years of prison, and twelve years serving Pharaoh. All that time, God was working to fulfill the promise in the dream God had given Joseph as a teen.

"...[love] keeps no record of being wronged." 1 Corinthians 13:5 (NLT).

Before God could use Joseph to save his family, Joseph had to love them enough to forgive them. The most stunning accomplishment of Joseph's extraordinary life was when he forgave his brothers. Love forgives.

"Love never gives up, never loses faith, is always hopeful, and endures through every circumstance." 1 Corinthians 13:7 (NLT).

Joseph never gave up, never lost hope. How do I know that? He served Potiphar faithfully. He wasn't sullen, depressed, angry or bitter. He became the head of Potiphar's household. He earned Potiphar's respect and trust. Not an easy thing for a slave to do. In prison, he did the same thing. He was placed in charge of his fellow prisoners. Joseph had every excuse to be discouraged, angry and bitter. God's love sustained Joseph through unimaginable adversity. God's love compelled Joseph to never give up, never lose faith, always be hopeful, and endure every circumstance.

Joseph overcame by outgrowing his circumstances.

The character God formed in him lifted Joseph out of his circumstances. Joseph wasn't sulking in a corner, planning his revenge on his brothers or imagining strangling Potiphar's lustful, lying wife. Joseph was loving others even when he was caged like an animal.

Joseph's "break" came because he was still serving others while in an impossible situation himself. Joseph had interpreted a dream for Pharaoh's cupbearer when he was in prison. The cupbearer told Pharaoh about Joseph's ability to interpret dreams. Joseph explained

Pharaoh's dream and gave Pharaoh a plan to prepare for the famine. Pharaoh made Joseph second in command of all of Egypt.

When adversity strikes, we cry out, "God, save me. God, take this away."

All we see is the pain, the adversity. God sees more than your pain and your problems. There's a lot more at stake in your life than you. That was true for Joseph, and it's true for you.

This is How We Overcome

Adversity crashes through the door of all of our lives, never welcome and rarely expected. Everyone faces hardship and adversity at some point in our lives.

1. **We Overcome by Faith.** Much adversity is NOT from God. God's response to that is to empower us, by faith, to fight and overcome that adversity.

> For every child of God defeats this evil world, and we achieve this victory through our faith.
> 1 John 5:4 (NLT)

2. **We Overcome by Character – Christlikeness**. God allows some adversity in our lives. He may even test us to make us stronger. In these times, God's provision for us is to allow the adversity and to empower us to grow so strong in Christ that we overcome by the character He has formed in us.

> But the Holy Spirit produces this kind of fruit in our lives: love, joy, peace, patience, kindness, goodness, faithfulness, gentleness, and self-control.

Galatians 5:22-23 (NLT)

> God's promise to Joseph purged his character
> until it was time for his dreams to come true.
> Psalm 105:19 (TPT)

Whether by faith or by Christlike character,
we overcome!

Activation

Think of a difficulty you either are facing right now
or recently went through. Approach God about
that situation.

When adversity comes, our first prayer is, "God remove
this." God's reply may be, "No, I need you to grow
character that enables you to overcome by love." God is
love. So, our character needs to begin there too.

I've tried to pray away some things that God put in
my life. That didn't go very well. Some of the dreams
God has given me were delayed until I learned to
love. I still find it hard to love people who oppose
me. But I'm learning to let the Holy Spirit replace my
character with His.

Sometimes we need to exercise our faith, sometimes
we need to grow more like Christ, and sometimes we
need both. If we know what is holding us back, we will
know how to move forward. So, ask.

*Jesus, I know that God's divine power has given me
everything I need for life and godliness (2 Peter 1:3).* **Is
this adversity for me to overcome by faith or are You
going to grow my character to overcome by love?**

Then ask, "Jesus, *what is your provision for me in this circumstance?*" Write down what he tells you. Lean into it. That's where your breakthrough will come.

Day 12 Jesus Calls, "Train Your Heart to Listen When I Speak"

> My heart has heard you say, "Come and
> talk with me."
> And my heart responds, "Lord, I am coming."
> Psalm 27:8 (NLT)

I'm looking for You, Jesus

I was 32, a recovering alcoholic, and a new Christian living in Tallahassee, Florida. I wanted to really know Jesus. I'd been reading everything about Jesus I could get my hands on. I was learning about Him, but I didn't know Him. I asked Jesus to take me out of my busy, townhouse-on-a-golf-course, lawyer life so I could get to know Him. He sent me to China. I didn't see that coming! But I went to China to meet Jesus.

Frank's Story

In August of 1989, I arrived in Guangzhou, China. I taught business and law at a small school north of the city. My search for a relationship with Jesus began in earnest. In the Spring of 1990, my friend, Frank, had an experience that showed me how anxious Jesus is to have a relationship with us.

After months of talking about the meaning of life, Frank told me: "I really want to believe in God, but I just can't." He told me how his mother worshiped the goddess of mercy (Quan Yin) and how she had powers. His mother could make things move, coins dance, etc. His mother wouldn't like it, and he was a little afraid of the goddess of mercy. I told him to come back that night. I told him that because I didn't know what to say and I needed time to pray.

I prayed all afternoon, and I had this faint impression that might have been Jesus saying, "Ask me." When Frank returned that night, I said, "When you're out running or any time you are alone, ask Jesus, "Are You real?" Frank just looked at me. I told him that's what I felt Jesus said he should do. I could see he didn't like my suggestion very much. He made some small talk because he was a very polite young man, then he made an excuse and bolted out of my apartment.

The next day, after morning classes, someone hammered on the screen door to my apartment, yelling, "He's real! He's real!" I unlocked the door, and Frank burst into the room.

"What happened?"

"He's real! He's real!" Frank was so excited I had a hard time getting the story from him.

Frank didn't believe Jesus would answer him, so he didn't ask when he went for his evening run. In fact, he wasn't going to ask at all. He went back to the dorm room he shared with seven other guys and decided to just go to sleep. But he couldn't sleep. Finally, he silently asked, "Jesus, are You real?" Then he slept.

"I had a dream. I saw a man. It was Jesus." In his dream, Frank and Jesus talked for a while, and Jesus told Frank a lot of things about himself and God. Frank explained to me what Jesus said.

I don't know who was more surprised, Frank or me. I then sat down, and we talked more about what Jesus told him. Frank knew about the Bible, but it was illegal to publish the Bible in China at that time. He had never read the Bible. I showed Frank, in the Bible, the things that Jesus told him. Everything Jesus told Frank in the dream was in the Bible. Frank prayed and gave his life to Jesus.

Jesus is real. And He talks to us.

I'm here.

I was in awe of Frank's experience. Jesus had never talked to me like that – in a dream or otherwise. But that was what I wanted. Frank's experience made me want it more.

The next semester, I taught at a college in Beijing. There was an International Fellowship in Beijing. I met some amazing Christians there. Over the next two years, I went all over Beijing asking missionaries, "Do you hear God?" "How do you experience Jesus?"

People thought that was strange. I didn't think that was strange. Do you think that was strange? I developed a reputation. Some "friends" even tried to warn the beautiful woman who is now my wife about me, "He asks strange questions! He thinks we should talk to Jesus." I still do.

To be honest, I was disappointed in what most people told me about hearing Jesus. But there were a few who listened and heard Him. I began to have precious times with Jesus, all alone, in my room at a small college over an hour north of the heart of Beijing. I felt His presence. He talked to me. Not conversations, but I began to "hear" Him more and more. He loved me. I didn't just know about Him; I met Him. He was real, tangible and undeniable. Over time, I learned to know His voice and the ways He "spoke" to me.

My Sheep Know My Voice

If you are a Christian, You hear Jesus.

> "My sheep listen to my voice; I know them, and they follow me."
> John 10:27 (NLT)

You are a Christian today because you heard His voice. Keep listening. He's still speaking.

Train Your Heart to Listen When I Speak

I've read quite a few books on hearing God. Dick Eastman, wrote an amazing book about the story of a prayer movement he launched: *The Purple Pig and Other Miracles*. In this book, Dick gives the most helpful insights I've seen on how to know you are hearing God. I share the gist of these insights below.[8]

1. **God still speaks to people today.**

The Bible makes scripture come alive. The Bible is the Holy Spirit talking to us. See Day 8 Jesus Calls, "Meet Me in My Word." In the Bible (e.g., 1 Kings 19) we learn that God sometimes talks to us in a "still, small, voice." To many, this is a "heart impression" or an "inaudible voice." You've probably experienced this. Most Christians I know have. In fact, many came to Christ by following this "still small voice."

To hear God, you need to believe that God speaks to people today.

---

[8] The Purple Pig and Other Miracles, Dick Eastman, page 108.

2. **God speaks from His dwelling place, the hearts of His children**.

The Holy Spirit lives in us once we are born again. So, it is only natural we would hear Him within ourselves.

> "… I will ask the Father, and he will give you another Advocate, who will never leave you. He is the Holy Spirit, who leads into all truth. The world cannot receive him, because it isn't looking for him and doesn't recognize him. **But you know him because he lives with you now and later will be in you.**" John 14:15–17 (NLT)

When Jesus died and was resurrected, men received the Holy Spirit to live in us.

> "Do you not know that **you are the temple of God and *that*** the Spirit of God dwells in you?" 1 Corinthians 3:16 (NKJ)

We all have a running dialog in our heads. When it is from God "it is a quiet thought or impression that flows out of one's heart and into his or her mind."[9]

3. **God gives us the privilege and the responsibility of hearing His voice.**

Jesus calls us His flock. He doesn't drive us like you drive cattle. He walks ahead of us, and we follow Him. How can we follow Him? Because we know His voice.

> After he has gathered his own flock, he walks ahead of them, and they follow him because they know his voice.

---

[9] The Purple Pig and Other Miracles, Dick Eastman, p 106.

> "My sheep listen to my voice; I know them, and they follow me."
> John 10:27 (NLT)

Jesus wants us to walk with Him every day. And He has terrific plans, great adventures for our lives. Without Him, we can do nothing. With Him, we can do anything. As you are walking with Jesus, He WILL talk to you. He will encourage you. And He will tell you what to do. He may even correct you, firmly but lovingly. We have the privilege and responsibility of hearing and knowing His voice.

4. **If you want to continue to hear from Jesus, do what He told you to do.**

You may have to learn this the hard way. I did. Once Jesus tells you something, act on it. If you don't, He may just quietly wait for you to obey. Quietly. I've had times when I couldn't hear Him. I asked why and suddenly I remembered what He told me to do. I did it. Then I heard Him speaking to me again.

> 'Obey me,' says the Lord, 'so I can do for you the wonderful things I swore I would if you obeyed'
> Jeremiah 11:5 (TLB)

5. **Silencing other voices.**

There are three voices we can hear in our heads: our own voice, Satan's, and God's.

Our path to silencing other voices is found in James: "Submit yourselves, then, to God. Resist the devil, and he will flee from you." James 4:7 (NIV)

Submit yourselves to God. True submission will silence "self."

Resist the devil, and he will flee from you. The Bible gives us authority over the devil. Take it.

Pray, *"Lord, it's not what I want. I give up what I want. I submit to Your will. Satan, be quiet. Lord, I only want to hear Your voice."*

6. Does it sound like Jesus?

Matthew, Mark, Luke, John, and Acts give us a very clear picture of who Jesus is. We see His patience, His compassion, and how He treated people who were despised and condemned in His culture. Jesus continuously saw people as who they could be, not who they were. You can expect Him to talk to you like that.

We can read the words He spoke. We see Him talking to his disciples, upset family members, a prostitute, thieves, lepers, a woman caught in adultery, and religious leaders.

The same Jesus will talk to you. Everything Jesus says to you will always be consistent with the Bible, with Jesus' character and heart. Jesus will sound like the Jesus you find in the Bible. He still has the same "voice."

When I first began to hear His voice, I sometimes wasn't sure. So, I asked Him to confirm what He had said. He did, often by showing me scripture. He doesn't mind repeating Himself if we really want to know it is Him. Many times, that confirmation came from other people. Many times, I haven't mentioned what Jesus told me before they say Jesus told them the same thing.

Now, you can listen with confidence that you will hear Jesus, know His voice and follow Him. It gets much easier with practice.

Activation

Asking Jesus personal questions is a great way to practice hearing His voice. Ask the question below and then write down what you heard, saw or what He impressed on your heart.

Ask Him, "Jesus, what do you like most about me today?"

Day 13 Jesus Calls, "Meet Me in Prayer."

> Our common ideas regarding prayer are not found in the New Testament. We look upon prayer simply as a means of getting things for ourselves, but the biblical purpose of prayer is that we may get to know God Himself.
> - Oswald Chambers

Pray for Barney

I first met Barney when I spoke to his Seniors Sunday School class at my church in Tallahassee, Florida. I was going to China to teach at a university for a year. Barney was one of several people who said they would pray for me. I wrote down their addresses and sent newsletters every month. This was in 1989, long before text messages and e-mail. Back then, it took at least two weeks to send a letter, another two to get an answer – if the mail made it through. A lot of letters didn't.

Barney did pray for me. And he was one of the few people who actually wrote. I came to love Barney and his newsy letters.

One day, I was alone in my small apartment north of Beijing, when Jesus suddenly told me to pray for Barney. That was unusual for me at the time. I wasn't hearing Jesus very clearly yet, but this was clear. And urgent! I somehow knew Barney was in trouble - big trouble.

I began to pray. I sensed physical danger. It was urgent! It felt so heavy. Jesus didn't tell me what it was. But I could sense Barney was in great danger. I prayed hard, and I didn't stop until I felt a deep peace. Barney was going to be okay. I was as sure of that as I was sure he had been in trouble.

I wrote Barney a letter and asked him what happened on that date and time. Several weeks later I got a short note from Barney. At the time Jesus told me to pray, Barney was getting emergency medical attention for his heart. He was reluctant to talk about it, but from what he wrote it sounded like a heart attack. He was shocked that I knew. Me too.

Since then, Jesus has called me to pray for specific people and situations many, many times. Prayer is the place of meeting Jesus in His love for us and others. It is the place where we learn His heart and pray His desires into reality.

Prayer is the meeting place of love.

Jesus invites us to come to the place of His love: prayer. We come to meet with Jesus, the intercessor. We come to be loved and receive His love for others and from that love, we pray.

I struggled all day to write this devotional. Jesus used the time to make me rethink prayer, not the mechanics of prayer, but the heart of prayer. Tonight, as I was finishing writing, I heard Him say, "Prayer, genuine heartfelt prayer is a tremendous act of love."

Prayer is two-way love. In love, Jesus calls you to meet Him in prayer. Jesus knows more about prayer than anyone. He continually intercedes between us and God.

> Therefore He is able also to save forever (completely, perfectly, for eternity) those who come to God through Him, since He always

> lives to intercede and intervene on their
> behalf [with God].
> Hebrews 7:25 (AMP)

Intercede means "to act... on behalf of someone in difficulty or trouble."[10]

Jesus sits on a throne at the right hand of God. From that throne, Jesus acts on behalf of each of us in our difficulties and troubles.

The throne is Jesus authority as God. God didn't just give Jesus specific authority over the earth. Jesus died for that. After living a perfect life as a man, Jesus died and was raised to life because death exists only in those who sin. Jesus, the man, never sinned. God sentenced Satan for the murder of Jesus. God gave Satan's authority over the earth to Jesus. And God declared that the same Holy Spirit who raised Jesus from the dead would raise to life all who love Jesus and submit to Him as Savior and Lord. Jesus is sitting at the right hand of God, interceding to enforce His victory in our lives.

In love, Jesus calls you to meet Him in prayer.

> Enter his gates with thanksgiving and his
> courts with praise; give thanks to him and
> praise his name.
> Psalm 100:4 (NIV)

Your spirit enters the gates of the Kingdom of God with thanksgiving. You lovingly thank Jesus in response to who He is and all He's done in His love for you. "Thank You, Jesus."

---

[10]https://www.dictionary.com/browse/intercede

You praise and worship Jesus and Father God. Suddenly, you are in His courts, boldly approaching His throne of grace and mercy to get help in time of need. You are bold because you belong here. Much-loved sons and daughters are welcome in the throne room. You smile at Father God. He looks at you, love burning in His eyes. He's so proud of you. He waits expectantly to hear what is on your heart. You nod to Jesus, the best brother ever, your best friend, and prayer partner.

> So whenever we are in need, we should come bravely before the throne of our merciful God. There we will be treated with undeserved kindness, and we will find help.
> Hebrews 4:16 (CEV)
>
> Therefore let us [with privilege] approach the throne of grace [that is, the throne of God's gracious favor] with confidence *and* without fear, so that we may receive mercy [for our failures] and find [His amazing] grace to help in time of need [an appropriate blessing, coming just at the right moment]. Hebrews 4:16 (AMP)

As the physical you praises here on earth, the spirit that is you arrives at His throne. The scripture is true. God is enthroned on the praises of His people.

Love Activates Faith, Is Expressed through Faith, and Is the Place from which Faith Works

In the meeting place of prayer, we receive love and are changed. We become capable of giving love to God and to men. That love activates faith. The two become inseparable. In the process of being loved, we learn to love. We believe and trust in God's love for us and others. We learn his character and his intentions. Then we intercede. We act on behalf of those in difficulty or trouble: ourselves, our friends, family, even people we don't know. Jesus' love compels us to act: to pray. And our prayers are bold because they come from the heart of God.

> For [if we are] in Christ Jesus neither circumcision nor uncircumcision means anything, but only **faith activated** and **expressed** and **working through love**.
> Galatians 5:6 (AMP)
> When we are in Christ Jesus, ·it is not important if we are circumcised or not [L neither circumcision nor uncircumcision accomplishes anything]. The important thing is faith—the kind of faith that works through love.
> Galatians 5:6 (EXB)

These Three

God's love poured into our hearts activates both hope and faith for ourselves and others. These three work together. If one is weak, look for the other two. But it all begins with love. The greatest of these is love.

> Now remain these three: faith hope and love but the greatest of these is love.
> 1 Corinthians 13:13 (NIV)
> And hope does not put us to shame, because God's love has been poured out into our hearts through the Holy Spirit, who has been given to us.
> Romans 5:5 (NIV)

Love turns our hopes into faith.

Prayer begins in love. Not some will-of-the-wisp fanciful idea, but the tangible, reliable, rock-solid love of Jesus. A love that never fails and never fades.

Often, we are driven to prayer because of fear or pain. The dreaded phone call in the middle of the night. A panic attack. Depression. A disaster. No matter what causes you to pray, don't pray alone. Don't pray the problem. Go to Jesus. He is waiting to partner in prayer with you.

Follow the familiar path of thanksgiving to enter the gates of the Kingdom of God. Use your privilege as a son or daughter to enter God's courts, his throne room, with praise and worship. Boldly come to the throne of grace and mercy where you will find help in time of need.

Stay there. Let Jesus love you. In the presence of love, hope and faith will come. They live and work in love. That's why Satan tries so hard to create fear and depression in our lives. Once you feel loved, you will soar above the situation on the dual wings of hope (expectancy) and faith (trust and belief).

See Day 24 Jesus Calls, "Come Up Here," for practical steps to praying when overwhelmed by adversity.

Activation:

Pray this prayer.

Jesus, the next time I come stumbling into the throne room covered in fear, lies, and doubt, remind me how much you love me. Remind me that if Father God asked You to give Your life for me, how will He not give me anything else that I need?

Love reminds me of who You are and how much You have done for me. Love lifts me above my pain – physical and emotional. Love casts out fear. When I feel I have no hope, when faith seems beyond my grasp, I will fill myself with Your love. I will thank You and praise You. I will draw near to You and You will draw near to me. I will feel Your love. Your love gives me hope. Your love turns hope into faith. And faith moves mountains. I stand on these scriptures.

> Submit yourselves, then, to God. Resist the devil, and he will flee from you. Come near to God and he will come near to you.
>
> James 4:7-8 (NIV)
>
> Truly I tell you, if you have faith as small as a mustard seed, you can say to this mountain, 'Move from here to there,' and it will move. Nothing will be impossible for you."
>
> Matthew 17:20 (NIV)

Now, go meet Jesus and pray for someone on your heart.

Day 14 Jesus Calls, "Avoid Life's Drift."

> For this reason, **we must pay closer attention to the things we have heard, or we may drift away**.
> Hebrews 2:1 (ISV)
> I'll never forget what you've taught me, Lord, but when I wander off and lose my way, come after me, for I am your beloved!
> Psalm 119:176 (TPT)

The Great Drift

I'm going to say a word. Tell me the mental picture you see. "Drifting."

What did you see? I saw myself drifting down the Suwannee River on an inner tube. I was with friends, and we were relaxed, laughing, joking and splashing from time to time as someone dozed off. I did that a long time ago.

That's one kind of drift – just letting life take you where it will. It's great for a day of fun on a river, but not as a lifestyle.

In today's world, drift often looks more like a ship that has slipped its anchor and is being tossed to and fro on angry waves as the ship is driven toward a rocky shore. It's chaotic, demanding, and urgent. That's the kind of life most of us live today.

Drift could be something entirely different for you. What causes you to lose focus and momentum in your life?

Whether your drift is just going with the flow, being driven here and there by a frantic lifestyle, or a tragedy or misfortune that you never recover from, it's easy to drift through life. Then, one day you wake up. You take a long look at yourself in the mirror, and say, "What have I done with my life?"

We need Anchors

> Fearing that we would be dashed against the rocks, they dropped four anchors from the stern and prayed for daylight.
> Acts 27:29 (NIV)

Think of anchors. We know what they do. They hold us fast. In a choppy sea or a raging river, they hold us firm, preventing us from being tossed about on the waves of life or, worse, being dashed against the rocks of adversity.

> So that we are no longer children [spiritually immature], tossed back and forth [like ships on a stormy sea] and carried about by every wind of [shifting] doctrine....
> Ephesians 4:14 (AMP)

Anchors imply that we aren't moving forward, making progress. But step back and look at a small boat anchored against a raging storm. Step far out into space and look down at the earth. The anchor is attached to the earth which is moving around the sun. You don't feel like you are moving, but you are. The earth moves almost 30 kilometers a second, that's 67,000 miles an hour every day, all day as it goes around the sun.

Being anchored to Jesus is like that. When you are firmly anchored to Him, the currents of this world won't toss you around anymore. Your anchor will hold you firm. The winds and the currents will still beat against you. But He will hold you firm.

You will never do more, never go farther or faster than when you are anchored – heart-connected, to Jesus. When He moves, you will move with Him, your heart firmly anchored to His. And together, you will go far and do things you can't even imagine, let alone do on your own.

Anchor yourself to the One so much greater than you that you are like a small boat firmly anchored to the bottom of the ocean of a planet that is racing through space and time.

Securing Your Anchor in Jesus

1. The Anchor of Meeting Jesus in His Word

The Bible reveals Jesus. It reveals who God says you are. As you read the Bible the Holy Spirit reads you – He reveals to you what you can't see on your own: the deep things hidden in your heart.

So, don't be surprised when you open the Bible and find a scripture that gives you exactly what you need for the greatest crisis in your life. The Holy Spirit wrote the original words. He lives in those words. And He lives in you. He knows exactly who you are and what you need. He speaks the Living Word into your situation, your problem, or your need.

Grasp this, and it will change your life: the Bible is the Holy Spirit speaking to you. Meet him there.

> **Every Scripture has been written by the Holy Spirit, the breath of God.** It will empower you

by its instruction and correction, giving you the strength to take the right direction and lead you deeper into the path of godliness.

2 Timothy 3:16 (TPT)

2. The Anchor of Meeting Jesus in Praise and Worship

Thanksgiving takes us through the gates of God's kingdom. Praise ushers us into the throne room of God where Jesus is seated at Father God's right hand. Praise brings us into His presence. I love rowdy praise times. There is something amazing about praising God with wild abandon. You don't worry about what anyone is thinking about you. Self dies in praise. Your mind is renewed in Praise and Worship. You begin to see things the way Jesus does. You feel His love, and that changes everything.

> Enter his gates with thanksgiving; go into his courts with praise. Give thanks to him and praise his name.
>
> Psalm 100:4 (NLT)

Worship is our response to God's presence. Praise turns to Worship when God's presence fills the room. God's presence inspires awe. Everything calms down. My favorite times are when everyone suddenly grows silent. I've been in crowds of hundreds of people praising loudly one moment and the next you could hear a pin drop. Silence. No one said anything. God showed up.

You fall on your face in the presence of His holiness. Enveloped in His presence, you feel things lifting off of your – burdens, sins, and brokenness - emotional wounds are being healed. Bodies are healed. You do nothing. You just stay there and enjoy being loved, really, truly loved.

> So all of us who have had that veil removed
> can see and reflect the glory of the Lord. And
> the Lord—who is the Spirit—makes us more
> and more like him as we are changed into his
> glorious image.
> 2 Corinthians 3:18 (NLT)

3. The Anchor of Meeting Jesus in Prayer

In prayer, we learn to see people as Jesus does. We feel His heart for us and for others. His love compels us to do something about everything that is wrong around us. Through prayer, we can change the world. Our prayer life with Jesus becomes something greater than ourselves. Nothing is more energizing than being part of something greater than ourselves. Meeting Jesus in prayer changes the world, but it also changes us. And the greatest change of all is spending time with Jesus, touching the people of this world with His love. We learn to see others as He sees and feel His heart for them.

> For it is Christ's love that fuels our passion
> and motivates us because we are absolutely
> convinced that he has given his life for all of us.
> 2 Corinthians 5:14 (TPT)

What you do in a crowd, you can do one on one.

I meet with Jesus every morning to overcome the chronic pain I've had for over a decade. Pain would rob me of God's plans for my life – my destiny. I fight for my mornings. I have prolonged times with Jesus until he lifts me above the pain. If I don't spend that time with

Him, I will drift through the day, driven and harassed by pain. In Christ, I overcome – one morning at a time.

One day soon, I will be able to tell you that I am free from pain. I have the Lord's promise. In the meantime, what Satan meant to destroy me has made me run to Jesus every morning and stay there. I wouldn't trade the thousands of hours I've spent with God this last decade for anything!!

> And we know that God causes everything
> to work together for the good of those who
> love God and are called according to his
> purpose for them.
> Romans 8:28 (NLT)

Activation

What is the drift in your life? Be specific. Identify it. Ask Jesus to help you break free from the current of that drift so you can live a full, rich life.

Meet Jesus first thing every morning, and His anchor will hold you fast. Secure your anchor to Jesus all day by meeting Him in praise, in His Word, and in prayer. And you will find that you aren't standing still; you are walking with Him, hand in hand, toward the dream He has for your life.

Commit to Jesus what you are going to do to stop the drift. Make it simple, something you can begin **right now**. Write it out. Put it where you will see it first thing every morning and throughout your day. You're going to have a great day! String one great day to another, then another, and you will look back on a great life.

B. Become Like Jesus

God's plan from the very beginning was for us to be like Him. We were made in His image. After Adam and Eve chose to follow Satan, people began to be corrupted. Through Jesus, God made a way for us to become like Him again. The transformation of a person who has walked in deep darkness to a son of light is a sight to behold. The next eight devotionals are a path to how God changes us – heart transformation. He changes us from the inside out.

The greatest limitation in our lives is who we are. Sometimes God has to hold us back from our destiny because we haven't yet developed the Christ-like character to carry that destiny. Who we are determines what we are able to do. Follow the path to become like Christ.

Day 15 Jesus Calls, "Let me Transform You Into a New Person by Changing the Way You Think."

> Don't copy the behavior and customs of this world, but **let God transform you into a new person by changing the way you think**. Then you will learn to know God's will for you, which is good and pleasing and perfect.
> Romans 12:2 (NLT)

You Can't Change What You Can't See

In the summer of 1989, God answered my desperate prayer: "Let me work for You full time, so I won't ever go back." I was an alcoholic, fighting my way back to sanity after ten years of mind-twisting addiction. Addicts are some of the most twisted people on earth. Such is the power of drugs – for me, alcohol. The greatest barrier most alcoholics face is denial. At first, I denied alcohol was a problem. Then, when I knew it was, I denied that there was an answer. Even after I stopped drinking, my mind refused to accept who I had become as a person. I was about to find out.

I was in Pasadena, California, at William Carey University, taking an intensive training program to prepare me to teach law and business for a year – in China. China had been completely closed to foreigners for forty years when it reopened in the early 1980s. Life there was tough by American standards – physically and culturally. Our training was more like a boot camp, with lots of stress built in. Intentionally. Let's just say that everyone in the training quickly revealed who we were.

The Christian sending organization knew how tough the culture and daily life could be for us. So, they put us in teams of two. Each team would teach at a university in a major city. Teams were based on our choices for teammates (1st choice, 2nd, etc.) and our education and skills.

The selection process didn't go well. The administrator finally told us that there was one of us that no one wanted to be on their team. He began individual interviews to work out a compromise. I was the last one interviewed. He asked me to be the teammate of the guy who was my last choice. Poor guy, I thought. No one wanted him. I asked if there wasn't another option. In frustration, the administrator told me, "It's you. No one wants you on their team."

Transformation begins when the veil of deception is removed.

I sat there in stunned silence. And for the first time in years, the veil lifted off my eyes, and I saw who I had become. I had gone from being the president of my law school class to someone no one wanted to work with. As painful as that moment was, it was the beginning of my transformation. The stronghold of denial was broken off my life, and I invited God to change me to be like Jesus.

A year later, I returned to Pasadena to help train a new group of teachers. I was home for the summer, but going back to China in the fall. The head of the sending organization introduced me as the person who was the most transformed of anyone who had gone to China in my year.

Transformation begins when the veil of deception is removed. Only Jesus can do that.

When the veil is removed, we can see. My problem wasn't that I didn't want to see. My problem was I couldn't see. I couldn't see who I was. And because we all see others through our own lens, I couldn't see others clearly either.

> Satan, who is the god of this world, has blinded the minds of those who don't believe. They are unable to see the glorious light of the Good News. They don't understand this message about the glory of Christ, who is the exact likeness of God.
>
> 2 Corinthians 4:4 (NLT)
>
> So all of us who have had that veil removed can see and reflect the glory of the Lord. And the Lord—who is the Spirit—makes us more and more like him as we are changed into his glorious image.
>
> 2 Corinthians 3:18 (NLT)

Let Me Transform You.

In those early years in China, I didn't understand how God was changing me. My self-awareness, as you've already seen, was next to nonexistent. I just desperately loved Jesus and I wanted to be like Him. So, He changed me. At times, it was painful. Other times, He changed me without me even knowing it. But the change was profound. I still have a long way to go, but now I know what is possible.

Since then, I have worked as a life coach, home group leader, and teacher trainer. I needed to understand more how we change – for others and myself. What is the process? Wouldn't it help if we knew the process? Couldn't we cooperate more with God if we knew what He was doing?

So, I began praying. I prayed Moses' prayer, "If you are pleased with me, teach me your ways so I may know you and continue to find favor with you." Exodus 33:13 (NLT)

Jesus answered me. He replied, "Replacement." He showed me Ezekiel 36:26. God's way of changing us isn't like ours. *We try to change by changing what we do. God changes us by changing who we are.* God's change is heart change. And Ezekiel 36:26 makes it clear that God is the one doing it: "I will give you a new heart."

> I will give you a new heart and put a new spirit in you; I will remove from you your heart of stone and give you a heart of flesh.
> Ezekiel 36:26 (NIV)

What does that look like?

> Don't copy the behavior and customs of this world, but **let God transform you into a new person by changing the way you think**. Then you will learn to know God's will for you, which is good and pleasing and perfect.
> Romans 12:2 (NLT)
> For **it is [not your strength, but it is] God who is effectively at work in you, both to will and to work** [that is, strengthening, energizing, and creating in you the longing and the ability to fulfill your purpose] for His good pleasure.

Philippians 2:13 (AMP)

Three Keys to Personal Transformation

1. **God is the one doing the change.** You don't have godliness to install in yourself. Only God can give you that. Philippians 2:13 brings clarity: God works in you the desire and the ability to change. So, if you want to change, you do that by going to Him.

2. **God initiates; we respond.** He transforms us; we let Him. That also means we can stop Him. The greatest hindrance to us becoming who God dreamed of before we were born may be our reluctance to be changed. If you ask Him, he will give you the longing, the desire - the will to change (Philippians 2:13, above). Isn't that good news?

3. **Transformation is relational.** In other words, this is between you and Jesus. Here's how it has worked in my life. When I was born again, Jesus began showing me the wonderful things He had for me. I found most of them while reading the Bible. As I delighted in those things, Jesus gave them to me. Often it is a process where He replaces my junk with Himself.

> Praise the Lord, O my soul...who **satisfies your desires with good things**....
> Psalm 103:1, 5 (NIV)
> **Delight** yourself **in the Lord**, and **he will give you the desires of your heart**.
> Psalm 37:4 (ESV)

Activation Prayer

Lord, I've tried to change myself again and again. I've even been angry with myself because I couldn't be who I should be. I see it now. Jesus, without You, I can do nothing. But with You, I can do anything. Jesus, I'm asking You to lead me in the process of becoming more and more like You.

I want people to look at me and see You. I want to be Your message, written on a human heart.

So, open my eyes to the possibilities of my life. Let me dream again. Create in me desires only You can fill. Then fill them with Yourself!

I love You, Lord, with all my heart. Have Your way in me! I will do what You tell me to do, so I can be who You made me to be.

Day 16 Jesus Calls, "Drive Out the Inhabitants in Your Land."

> "'But if you do not drive out the inhabitants of the land, those you allow to remain will become barbs in your eyes and thorns in your sides. They will give you trouble in the land where you will live."
> Numbers 33:55 (NIV)

No, I'm not talking about your neighbors. The inhabitants are the things that live in your mind and heart. Some of them have been trying to destroy you for years.

Your Mind is the Battlefield

> For though we live in the world, we do not wage war as the world does.
> **The weapons we fight with** are not the weapons of the world. On the contrary, they **have divine power to demolish strongholds**.
> **We demolish arguments and every pretension** that sets itself up against the knowledge of God, and we **take captive every thought to make it obedient to Christ**.
> 2 Corinthians 10:3-5 (NIV)

Sin obviously has to go. We know that. But there are other things that are very destructive in our lives. They are the enemy's strongholds. "Stronghold" simply means a place from which the devil can strongly hold people, think of a fort or fortress in your mind.

This passage is talking about thoughts. We have thousands of thoughts every day. Most thoughts are fleeting – they come, and they go. Those thoughts don't influence us much. But some thoughts control us. Some thoughts determine the course of our lives.

What are these thoughts that hold us strongly?

Belief- a state or habit of mind in which trust or confidence is placed in some person or thing.[11]

Beliefs are thoughts that we are convinced are true. We may not be able to prove it, but we believe them. Our beliefs exert powerful influence over our lives.

> Beliefs are the filters through which we see others, ourselves, and every aspect of life.
>
> Our core beliefs limit or expand the possibilities and potential we see – in ourselves, in others and in situations. Negative beliefs limit; positive beliefs expand. Think about that for a minute. Most of us wouldn't try something if we thought it was impossible. Once we realize what is possible, our world expands. Knowing Jesus opens amazing possibilities and potential in our lives.
>
> Our core beliefs define us. They become our identity – who we think we are.

Arguments and Every Pretension

What Phillips translates as "arguments" that we demolish, other translations call imaginations, reasonings, or theories. The arguments we need to

---

[11] https://www.merriam-webster.com/dictionary/belief

demolish are thoughts and ideas that aren't true, in other words: false beliefs.

All your life, the devil and his fallen angels have tried to destroy you. Jesus took back the devil's authority. Deception is the primary tool the devil uses to harm you.

Satan uses deception to keep us from God's plan for us. He uses people and circumstances to create false beliefs:

- that will keep you from a relationship with God through Jesus;

- that will blind you from knowing what Jesus is like, who you are (your identity as a son, a daughter of God), and how to become like Jesus; and

- about your destiny – the amazing things God has planned for you to do.

The Stronghold of Pride

The second stronghold in this verse is the attitude of pride – a dangerous false belief.

Satan was thrown from heaven because he wanted to be worshiped like God. Eve wanted to be like God, knowing both good and evil, so she ate the forbidden fruit. Adam did too.

Human pride is what makes so many people today believe there is no God. In their pride, they deeply believe life is all about them, and they are the ones who determine what is real and what is right. The first sin, trying to make yourself God, is rampant in the world today.

How Do We Form Beliefs?

Lisa was invited to a local church. She went. The pastor preached about Father God. The pastor kept saying God is like your father. She jumped up and ran down the aisle, hit the crash bar on the door and stumbled into the parking lot, blinded by tears and rage. This was all wrong! How could the pastor say that? Her father had abused her for years. She wanted nothing to do with a God who was like her father. All the pain of those years of abuse came back to her. Fathers can't be trusted. They will hurt you – again and again. What a horrible church! She didn't ever want to go back there.

This story is true. It happened at my church. Lisa was acting on her beliefs. She ran away to protect herself from the pain inflicted by her father. She rejected God, the Father, because at an early age she learned not to trust "father." My wife, Karen, on the other hand, had a wonderful father. Listening to the very same sermon, she would have felt the love of God because Daddy Chan was a man full of God's love.

Beliefs are formed when we have experiences that we give meaning to. From birth, we are making meaning of what is happening. That's why three-year-olds ask, "Why?" every five minutes. They're trying to understand, to make meaning of everything. We decide the meaning of life based on our core beliefs, many of which we formed when we were quite young.

Some of these beliefs are wrong.

The parable of the wheat and tares explains this (Matthew 13:24-30). God plants truth in our lives. Satan plants tares - lies. Tares cannot be distinguished from wheat until the grain is ripe, ready to harvest.

The wheat produces grain, delicious and nutritious. Tares (darnel) are poisonous. Tares cause confusion or disorientation, dizziness and overall symptoms similar to being drunk. Tares confuse people, make them sick, and can even kill.

False beliefs look good, and they feel right. But the devil put them there to confuse you, disorient you, even destroy you. These are the strongholds we need to tear down. God will help!

How Can I Change Beliefs – My Own and Others'?

Most people believe that knowledge will change their beliefs. **Knowledge, even obvious truth, often isn't enough to change deeply-held beliefs.** Think politics. I'm constantly amazed that even when a false news report about a politician is completely debunked, people who strongly dislike that candidate still believe it. Knowledge isn't enough to change their minds. If they meet that person and have a good experience, that might change their mind.

Beliefs are formed when we have a powerful experience that we give meaning to. These experiences are often emotional because those are our most powerful experiences. They are also the ones we don't forget. We change what we believe only when we have experiences that contradict that belief.

To change false beliefs about God, we need to have experiences with God. What happened to Lisa? She did go back to that church. Lisa had some awesome experiences with God that challenged her false belief that all fathers are bad. Those experiences healed her and changed her view about Father God.

**Information about Jesus won't change you.
Experiencing Jesus will!**

We form beliefs to guide us, to protect us. We are slow to change what we believe. We protect our beliefs even long after they served their original purpose. Beliefs are most often changed by new experiences.

But we also are affected by the experiences other people have. When we hear a story and relate to it strongly, we often adopt that story as if it had happened to us. That's why we cry during movies or get nervous reading a good thriller. When something touches our emotions strongly, we experience it vicariously. The story becomes real to us, and we can even change what we believe because of a story.

I had read the research about stories changing beliefs, but it wasn't real to me until a young Chinese friend told me, "I decided to not believe in the God." We had talked about God before. I asked, "Why?" She told me she had watched the movie *The Da Vinci Code*. I tried to explain that the movie was fiction. She wasn't convinced. Her emotional experience trumped my facts.

The strongest influence on our beliefs is our experiences. Next, are stories that resonate – that connect with us on a heart level. We adopt those stories as if they were our own. So, if you want someone to believe in Jesus, bring them into an experience with Jesus or share stories about your experiences with Jesus.

Wait a minute. Doesn't Romans 10:17 say, "Faith comes by hearing and hearing by the word of God?" And faith is believing, right? So, people do believe from hearing the Bible. Yes, yes and yes. The Greek for "word" in

Romans 10:17 is "rhema" which means the "spoken word." It's the Holy Spirit speaking to us. The Bible isn't like any other book. It isn't just information. The Bible is alive. The Bible is the Holy Spirit speaking to us. We have experiences with God when we read the Bible looking for Him. (See Day 8 Jesus Calls, "Meet Me in My Word.")

Activation

One of the reasons false beliefs remain strongholds the devil can use to hold us back from Jesus is because we aren't aware they are there.

> The heart is deceitful above all things and beyond cure. Who can understand it? "I, the Lord, search the heart and examine the mind, to reward each person according to their conduct, according to what their deeds deserve."
>
> Jeremiah 17:9-10 (NIV)
>
> Search me, O God, and know my heart; test me and know my anxious thoughts. Point out anything in me that offends you, and lead me along the path of everlasting life.
>
> Psalm 139:23-24 (NLT)

Jesus, search my heart. Reveal the false beliefs that need to be removed. Give me experiences with You so I will KNOW the truth. And the truth will set me free to be with You, to become like You, and to do all that You have planned for my life.

Day 17 Jesus Calls, "I Will Make You Whole."

> May you experience the love of Christ.... Then you will be made complete with all the fullness of life and power that comes from God.
> Ephesians 3:19 (NLT)

Jesus came to destroy the work of the devil.

> The thief comes only in order to steal and kill and destroy. **I came that they may have and enjoy life, and have it in abundance [to the full, till it overflows]**.
> John 10:10 (AMP)
> The Son of God came for this: to destroy the devil's work.
> 1 John 3:8 (ERV)

The life God planned for you is this joyous, wonderful experience of being filled with all the good things of God – so full that you overflow on the people all around you. Jesus came to give you the life God dreamed you would live. And He did!

Satan came to steal, kill and destroy.

Remember who Satan is. He's a wicked angel who tried to take God's place. He wanted other angels to worship him. God threw him out of heaven. Jesus saw it. It was wild. Satan fell from heaven like lightning. Satan and one-third of the angels who foolishly followed him are stuck on earth. And he's angry. He can't hurt God, so he tries to hurt us as much as he can because he knows God loves us.

One more thing. Satan is persuasive. Can you imagine being in heaven, with God, seeing how awesome God is, and still deciding to follow Satan, not God? One-third of the angels did. Whoa! Crazy persuasive!

Satan came to steal your identity as a daughter or son of God and anything else he could get his hands on.

Satan came to kill. Satan deceived Eve and Adam to disobey God, and they died that day. Spiritually, they died. A short time later, one of their sons killed the other. Now, everything on earth dies. But it wasn't like that in the beginning.

Satan came to destroy: relationships and everything God has planned for your life, including hope, love, joy, peace and the influence God has planned for you to have on this earth.

In his first encounter with a man and a woman, Satan separated them from God - and each other. When God asked who ate the forbidden fruit, Adam said, "It was the woman." Can't you see his finger pointing? I wonder if they ever fought about that?

How Does Jesus Make Us Whole?

1. He reveals the true thoughts and motives of our hearts.

As we read the Bible, the Holy Spirit reveals to us the thoughts, motives, attitudes, and desires of our hearts. We see ourselves as we really are.

> For we have the living Word of God, which is full of energy, and it pierces more sharply than a soldier's sword. It will even penetrate to the very core of our being where soul and spirit,

bone and marrow meet— splitting them in two! It **interprets and reveals the true thoughts and motives of our hearts**.

There is not one person who can hide their thoughts from God, for nothing that we do remains a secret, and nothing created is concealed, but everything is exposed and defenseless before his eyes, to whom we must render an account

Hebrews 4:12-13 (TPT)

This is one of the most amazing scriptures in the Bible. As I read the Bible, I see what a godly life looks like. At the same time, the Holy Spirit is showing me what my life looks like compared to the Bible. He shows me where I am and where I can be. He invites me, "Come up here." And I say, "Yes. I want that." Then He shows me how and helps me make the climb.

2. **He replaces the old with the new.**

I struggled with some very rough edges to my character for years — especially anger. I felt so broken. And I was sure God wanted me to be whole. I had tried and tried to fix myself. I failed again and again. I was hurting the people I loved the most.

I remembered Moses' prayer, "If you are pleased with me, teach me your ways so I may know you and continue to find favor with you." Exodus 33:13 (NLT). What I was doing wasn't working so I asked Jesus how He would heal my brokenness. How would He make me whole?

Jesus told me "Replacement. I'm not here to fix you. I replace the old nature with the new," and He showed me Ezekiel 36:26.

> I will give you a new heart and put a new spirit in you; I will remove from you your heart of stone and give you a heart of flesh.
> Ezekiel 36:26 (NIV)

3. He changes us from the inside out. All real change is heart change.

I had been trying to change my actions, in particular, losing my temper. I wish I could tell you there was a "miracle moment" when everything changed. But there wasn't. I began having experiences with Jesus. He just loved me again and again. Over time and without me being aware of it, I became milder, gentler, and more patient.

> May you experience the love of Christ.... Then you will be made complete with all the fullness of life and power that comes from God.
> Ephesians 3:19 (NLT)

I saw this translation of Ephesians 3:19, and it hit me: love completes us. Yes, I had heard about the power of love, but it sounded so religious. Until I experienced it, it wasn't real to me.

There wasn't anything wrong with having a strong sense of right and wrong. God made me that way. I was a lawyer, and my passion for justice was my strength. God has an absolute sense of justice, but it is tempered by love.

Notice how God is both kind and severe. He is
severe toward those who disobeyed, but kind to
you if you continue to trust in his kindness. But
if you stop trusting, you also will be cut off.
Romans 11:22 (NLT)

What was missing in me was love.

What happened next is hard to explain. I was born
again. But I was still an angry young man. I had scars,
deep wounds. I began spending time with Jesus in
praise, in prayer, and in His Word. I felt His tangible
presence day after day. I felt His love. Words fail
to describe what these months were like. I began
journaling how Jesus was touching me and what He was
saying to me. I couldn't see it at the time, but over many
months Jesus was filling me with His love.

For years, my temper was uncontrollable. My anger
was so strong it overwhelmed everything. When I felt
hurt or threatened by others, I would explode in anger.
These explosions were followed by genuine regret and
shame. I desperately wanted to change.

Then it happened. Anger erupted over something my
wife said, but I realized love was there. I had a choice. I
was angry, but I could choose not to release it. I began
to choose love. It wasn't easy, but love was somehow
available. I was still upset, but I chose not to lose
my temper. Years later I can look back and see that
Jesus had filled me with His love so when I felt hurt or
threatened by others, I could choose His love over my
anger. Then, when I could choose, He convicted me of
unrighteous anger. His correction was an invitation to
share in His holiness – to become like Jesus.

> Our parents corrected us for the short time
> of our childhood as it seemed good to them.
> But **God corrects us** throughout our lives for
> our own good, **giving us an invitation to share
> his holiness.**
>
> Now all **discipline** seems to be more pain than
> pleasure at the time, yet later it **will produce a
> transformation of character,** bringing a harvest
> of righteousness and peace to those who
> yield to it.
> Hebrews 12:10-11 (TPT)

The brokenness that we still have in our lives is made
whole by being loved by Jesus. Satan and the world
have abused us, but Jesus' love is what heals and
completes us. What is wrong in our lives is made right
only by the experience of being loved by Jesus.

Activation

Invite Jesus to meet you in the area of your life where
you are most broken. It could be a poor self-image,
impatience, pride or something horrible someone
did to you....

*Jesus, I am convinced that Your love will complete me in
this area of my life. Come, touch this brokenness in me.*

> May you experience the love of Christ.... Then
> you will be made complete with all the fullness
> of life and power that comes from God.
> Ephesians 3:19 (NLT)

*Touch my emotional wounds here (list one or two points
of your emotional pain). Jesus, I believe Ephesians 3:19.*

Your love will heal and complete me. Jesus, fill each emotional wound with Your love.

If your brokenness is a broken relationship, pray: *Jesus, heal and restore godly relationships with …. (name them).*

I repent of sin (list, if any) in this area. Help me to not sin again.

Heal and renew my thoughts and beliefs about…..

Thank You, Jesus, for letting me feel your love that will complete and make me whole.

Now, meet with Jesus every morning and let Him love you and make you whole.

Day 18 Jesus Calls, "You are Light of the World."

> "Your lives light up the world. Let others see your light from a distance."
> Matthew 5:14 (TPT)
> "You are the light of [Christ to] the world."
> Matthew 5:14 (AMP)
> "Make your light shine, so that others will see the good that you do and will praise your Father in heaven."
> Matthew 5:16 (CEV)

How powerful is the light coming from your life?

Every believer carries the light of the glory of the Gospel of Jesus. But what we do with the light we receive determines how bright the light of Christ in our lives appears to others.

Sunlight is amazing. It is a source of life for plants and all life on earth. It is a source of great beauty and inspiration. Sunlight is absolutely needed for life to exist on this planet. Natural sunlight is strong enough to push back the darkness of night and light up the half of the planet where it shines.

Jesus said you are the light of the World. You are a source of life for people who see His light in you.

Sunlight **magnified** creates heat. Have you ever used a magnifying glass and sunlight to set a piece of paper on fire? It doesn't take long.

> "Oh, magnify the LORD with me, and let us exalt his name together!"

Psalm 34:3 (ESV)

To magnify is to make greater in size or importance. Have you noticed that what you focus on becomes greater in your life? When we make God greater in our lives, God sets us on fire. People will come to watch us burn.

A laser is light that is concentrated again and again by adding energy. The wavelengths of that light become the same length. Scientists call this being "absolutely in step." Light that is concentrated (focused) and "absolutely in step" is a laser. Lasers are bright - able to shoot miles and miles into space and powerful enough to cut through thick steel.

> "Since we live by the Spirit, let us keep in step with the Spirit."
> Galatians 5:25 (NIV)

When we live our lives in such a way that we are "absolutely in step" with the Holy Spirit, we become radiant and powerful beyond description. We get "in step" by adding energy to our focus. When we do, God gives us more light (revelation, anointing, and godly character).

We get "absolutely in step" by coming to Jesus in absolute surrender. He gives us the Holy Spirit who comes to live in us to guide and empower us to walk step by step with Jesus. He guides. He empowers. We focus. We listen. We obey with passion and enthusiasm. And we become brilliant with His light as we are transformed into His likeness.

Arise, Shine, for Your Light Has Come.

> "Arise, shine, for your light has come,
> and the glory of the Lord rises upon you.
> See, darkness covers the earth
> **and thick darkness is over the peoples,**
> but the Lord rises upon you
> **and his glory appears over you.**
> Nations will come to your light,
> **and kings to the brightness of your dawn.»**
> Isaiah 60:1-3 (NIV**)**

Several years ago, I was a home fellowship leader in a great church in Hong Kong. One day, the Lord showed me a map of the Kowloon Peninsula, the part of Hong Kong we lived in, and He showed me points of light on a very dark map. The points of light were home fellowships.

I left Hong Kong ten years ago. But today, there are many "points of light" on a map of this church's home fellowships throughout Hong Kong. God was showing us the future. But he was also showing us Isaiah 60:1-3.

Darkness covers the earth. The darkness over people is worse; "thick darkness" covers the people. God's plan from the beginning was to fill the earth with His children – people made in His image, who thought and acted as He did. Adam and Eve interrupted that plan. Jesus came to make it a reality. Christians, born again, filled with the glory and goodness of God, covering the earth is God's plan. Each of us is a point of light, strategically placed by God to bring light to our families, our neighborhoods, our workplaces, schools, supermarkets....

People will be drawn to your light. Be bold. Be radiant.

Activation

Lord, I love Your light.

I want to be the bright light I was born to be.

*I commit to living a life of focus. Today I will focus on **being with You**, **becoming like You** and **doing things with You**, Jesus.*

Be With Jesus: *I will begin my day meeting with You, Jesus. Walk with me, Jesus. I want Your light to radiate from me as I spend time with You throughout the day.*

Become Like Jesus: *I want your light to shine through my character as I become like You. I want people to look at me and see You.*

Do What Jesus Wants to Do Together: *And I want to release Your light by doing everything you have for me to do today. The most difficult people in my life live in darkness; thick darkness is over their lives. Satan has blinded them, kept them in the dark. I want the joy of touching them with the light of Your love and the light of the glory of Your Gospel.*

Jesus, make me a blessing to someone today. Who needs me today? How can I serve them?

Day 19 Jesus Calls, "I give You My Authority."

> Jesus came and told his disciples, "**I have been given all authority in heaven and on earth. Therefore, go and make disciples of all the nations**, baptizing them in the name of the Father and the Son and the Holy Spirit. Teach these new disciples to obey all the commands I have given you. And be sure of this: I am with you always, even to the end of the age."
> Matthew 28:18-20 (NLT)

> Now you understand that **I have imparted to you all my authority to trample over his kingdom. You will trample upon every demon before you and overcome every power Satan possesses**. Absolutely nothing will be able to harm you as you walk in this authority.
> Luke 10:19 (TPT)

Authority – the Power to Influence or Command Thought, Opinion or Behavior

The Merriam Webster dictionary defines **authority**: *power to influence or command thought, opinion, or behavior.*[12]

The authority Jesus gives us is His power over demons and the ability to influence people – what people think, what they believe and what they do. Jesus tells us to go, disciple nations.

The earth is God's. He gave Adam dominion over the earth. Adam was tricked into giving his authority

---

[12] https://www.merriam-webster.com/dictionary/authority

to Satan. Jesus came as a man to take back man's authority. Jesus did that. And He gave that authority back to all who would accept Him and follow Him. You and I are powerful people.

You are God's Ekklesia

The Greek word "ekklesia" (often translated "church") appears in the King James New Testament 114 times. But Ekklesia isn't a religious word. It is a government word. It means an assembly - a council to govern the affairs of a city, region or nation. Ekklesia originally described the assembly of citizens of Greece who gathered to make decisions about government.

The Romans used a similar idea to settle conquered nations. The Romans realized that unless they changed the culture of a region, that region would always try to revert to their old culture. So loyal Roman citizens were given land in newly conquered regions and tasked with living there and establishing Roman lifestyle, culture, and government in that place. The goal was that, over time, the people would embrace the Roman way of life and see Rome as their nation. The ekklesia in a city was the ruling council made up of these Roman citizens.

This is what ekklesia meant to Jesus and the authors of the New Testament. The ekklesia in their towns and cities were ruling councils: a group of individuals, each with authority and responsibility.

So, why do we translate ekklesia as "church?" Great question. The word "church" did not appear at all in the first translation of the New Testament into English. "Ekklesia" was translated as "congregation."

William Tyndale finished the first translation of the
New Testament into English in 1525 while hiding from
Church authorities. The Bibles were printed in Germany
and smuggled into England because the Roman
Catholic Church prohibited translating the Bible into the
language of the people. The Church maintained that
Bibles were "holy" and that common men were too
simple to understand the truths of God. All Bibles used
in the Church were in Latin, a language no one spoke,
the language of the Church. Only priests could know and
tell the people what the Bible meant. Church services
(masses) were also done in Latin. People were required
to attend but were not allowed to understand. The
Church controlled people by placing priests and church
authorities between men and God.

In 1565 Tyndale was arrested, tried, strangled and
burned at the stake for making the Bible available to the
common people in a language they could understand.

King James of England made the Bible widely available
to the common people in 1611 because he wanted
to break the Roman Catholic Church's influence over
English people. With that political goal in mind, King
James gave the translators specific instructions.
The third instruction was: "The old ekklesiastical
words to be kept, as the word church, not to be
translated congregation."[13] He was saying, where it
says "congregation" you translate that as "church."
King James didn't want people to know the Bible gave
authority to us individually and that we are the church.
He wanted the Church of England to be the "ekklesia" in
the minds of the people.

---

[13] https://en.wikipedia.org/wiki/King_James_Version

For almost 400 years, most Bible translations followed the King James' Bible and translated "ekklesia" as "church." Today, in churches all around the world we are taught, "You are the church."

You Have the Authority of Jesus

What happens when we translate "ekklesia" as "congregation?"

You and I begin to realize that we each have Jesus' authority. And with that authority comes the ability to respond (responsibility) to the needs of our lost and dying world. *We realize we can make a huge difference. Just you. Even me.*

God has this amazing picture of each of us with the ability to influence the thinking, beliefs, and actions of our families, friends, coworkers, even people we pass on the street. We are influential people!

We have the power to pray and release people from deep darkness. We share God's Living Word and release light and life all around us. We can cooperate with Jesus, allowing Him to transform us, replacing our character with His, to the point that people look at us and see Him.

As we spend time in God's presence, we will go out into our communities and carry His presence with us. His presence will touch and change people. And in our daily lives, God will give us assignments. Help a friend pay the rent. Stop and listen to the lonely old man who lives on the corner. Pray for the cashier with arthritis in her knees.

God sees each of us establishing a zone of influence around us, building the Kingdom of God wherever we are. Why can we do all of this? We are the EKKLESIA of God. We live and breathe the authority of Jesus over all the earth.

Kingdom Authority

When most of us hear "authority," we think of governments, dictators, bad teachers, bad bosses, etc. Authority is often used to describe people who have power and use it for their own ends. Jesus came to earth to establish the kingdom of God. Authority has a different meaning in God's kingdom. In His kingdom, leaders serve.

> The greatest among you will be the one who always serves others from the heart.
> Matthew 23:11 (TPT)

July 10, 2012, I had this experience with God where He showed me the power of love.

> *I see a waterfall, of love. Continuous. Pounding. Driving. Wearing away the hardest rock. Over time. Washed in the water of his love, the hardness, the shell of men is worn off, eroded by the constant pounding flow of God's love. Men are like a solid layer of rock under a waterfall. Love wears away the rock. You can't see it at first. It takes time. It doesn't look powerful. The world has a distorted view, even portraying love as wimpy. But a constant stream of love is pure power. Hear the roar! It's the lion of Judah. The roar of the waterfall of love is the roar of God!* ***Love is the authority God gives us.***

I think of how many times Christians reached out and touched me over the years until I gave my heart to Christ. Many! Many! Each touch did its work – wearing away a little more of the hardness of my heart.

We need to learn to love so we can expand the kingdom of God here on earth. We are here to establish the reign of love on the earth.

For the love of Christ controls and compels us...
2 Corinthians 5:14 (AMP)

We are ruled by Christ's love for us. (CEV)

For the love of Christ puts us into action. (NLV)

For it is Christ's love that fuels our passion and motivates us, because we are absolutely convinced that he has given his life for all of us. This means all died with him, (TPT)

Activation

Pray this with me:

Jesus, I know that all authority in heaven and on earth has been given to You. And You send me into the world to touch the world with Your authority. I take my place in the ekklesia of God. I will take Your authority – the ability to influence thought, opinion and action by serving people with Your love.

I embrace the ministry of nudges. I will touch the people around me with Your love. I will fight for them in prayer. I will serve others as You did Jesus. Fill me with Your love so I will have more to give.

Jesus, make me a blessing to someone today. Show me who needs to be touched by Your love today. And help me love them as You would.

Make this a daily habit and your life will turn into an adventure. Jesus will have you touching people with His love everywhere you go. This is so much fun!

Day 20 Jesus Calls, "Revelation is an Invitation to An Encounter with Me."

When I was a new Christian (in my early 30's), my pastor preached a sermon about faith that rocked my world. The scripture he used burned in my heart. I heard his call to action: have faith. That's what I wanted more than anything in the world. But my pastor didn't tell us how.

So, while shaking hands on the way out of the church, I told him I loved the message. He beamed. I asked, "Uh, how can I do that?"

After several awkward moments of hemming and hawing, he said to just do it. I shouldn't ever play poker. Dismay was written all over my face. He saw this was important to me. He invited me to his office that week to talk about it. I went. He didn't have answers then either. I was shocked and dismayed.

I've heard dozens of messages like that over the years. Messages with a call to action, but not a clue as to the process of walking in that truth.

Practically how can I do that?

More recently, in a small group Sarah, a dear friend, was deeply troubled. The teaching shared that day was exactly what she needed. One of the verses taught that day clearly told her what to do, but not how. In tears, she said she wanted to do that, but didn't know how. She looked at our group and asked, "Practically, how can I do that?"

That's a great question. A Jesus question. Jesus didn't come to earth and live high above our daily problems. He chose to walk among us, staying in peoples' homes, sharing life with us. Jesus dealt with practical problems. He turned water into wine so a poor groom wouldn't be embarrassed by running out of wine at his wedding. Jesus turned a few pieces of flatbread and some fish into a banquet for 4,000 because they had been with him for three days and he was worried they might faint on the way home as some lived far away. Mark 8. Practical Jesus. Thoughtful Jesus.

Back to Sarah. Several well-meaning friends gave advice. Most of it was good general advice. Some was…. well, contradictory. And I noticed that the advice reflected the personality and character of the advice givers. Different people offered different answers. It was rather confusing. Sarah continued to weep.

And then I heard Jesus tell me that none of that was what Sarah needed. Jesus encouraged Sarah and told her to rest in Him. I told her what Jesus had said. You could feel the shift in the atmosphere in the room. Others confirmed what Jesus was saying to her. For Sarah, at that time, rest and trust in Jesus was His provision – His practical answer. Sarah stopped crying. Jesus had answered her question.

Human Answers Don't Work for Spiritual Problems

We are all wonderfully different people, and each of us is at a different place spiritually. What works for you today may not be good for you tomorrow because you will be at a different place in the path you are walking.

Jesus knows where we are in life. And He knows exactly what we need. Human answers don't work for spiritual problems. We need to hear from Him. Sarah needed to hear that this was one of those times that Jesus was going to work that scripture into her life. He needed her to rest in Him and trust Him to do the heavy lifting. Jesus reveals things in our lives so we will invite Him into that area of our life to help us there.

Revelation is an Invitation to an Encounter with Jesus

In other words, **revelation is an invitation to an encounter with Jesus.** He reveals things to us so we will meet Him there. My heart burned to have faith because Jesus would later call me to pray for others. I left the meeting with my pastor in the first story discouraged, but Jesus had birthed in me a great desire to have faith. I pursued that desire. That was the beginning of a long journey – one I'm still on. And Jesus did meet me there. Most of what I know about faith and prayer He taught me through experiences with Him.

> **Don't just listen to the Word of Truth and not respond to it, for that is the essence of self-deception**. So **always let his Word become** like poetry **written and fulfilled by your life!**
>
> If you listen to the Word and don't live out the message you hear, you become like the person who looks in the mirror of the Word to discover the reflection of his face in the beginning. You perceive how God sees you in the mirror of the Word, but then you go out and forget your divine origin. But those who set their gaze deeply into the perfecting law of liberty are fascinated by and respond to the truth they hear and are strengthened by it—they experience God's blessing in all that they do!

James 1:22-25 (TPT)

Use It or Lose It

Revelation is the invitation. If you don't respond, it will be lost. For forty years God fed the Israelites by manna falling from heaven six days a week. Manna left on the desert floor had to be collected early. It would be gone a few hours later, burned off by the hot desert sun. After they picked it up, they had to prepare it and cook it that day, overnight it would rot. (Exodus 16)

We have much better bread than the manna the Israelites had:

> Jesus said, "I am the living bread that came down from heaven." John 6:51 (ESV)
>
> But he [Jesus] answered, "It is written, "'Man shall not live by bread alone, but by every word that comes from the mouth of God.'" Matthew 4:4 (ESV)

How many times have you heard an amazing sermon and thought, *Wow, this is life-changing?* You knew it was from God; it was what you needed that day. Then you went to lunch with your friends after church, and for the next week, your life was a whirl of work, family, and activity. The next Sunday someone asked you "Wasn't last week's message amazing?" And you have trouble remembering what the message was. It was something about...

Revelation quickly fades unless you gather it, prepare it and digest it (put it in your heart). The proper response is to write down what Jesus shows you. Then invite Him to encounter you in that revelation. Ask Jesus to work it into your life.

It COULD have been life-changing. Revelation is an invitation to take the next step.

What Does This Mean? What Must I do?

In Acts chapter 2, we see the 120 followers of Jesus who were baptized in the Holy Spirit speaking in tongues and causing a scene. People recognized them as local people, but they were praising God in foreign languages. A crowd formed. From the crowd came two questions that are great questions to ask Jesus when He "reveals" something:

> Amazed and perplexed, they asked one another, **"What does this mean?"**
> Acts 2:12 (NIV)

Peter stood up and explained. And someone from the crowd asked the next, great Bible question – the same question my friend just asked, but in these words:

> When the people heard this, they were cut to the heart and said to Peter and the other apostles, "Brothers, **what shall we do?"**
> Acts 2:37 (NIV)

"What does this mean? What must I do?"

Why would God give you amazing secrets if you don't even respond to them? God reveals His secrets to his friends who will appreciate them and use them. That's you.

> My child, will you treasure my wisdom? Then, and only then, will you acquire it.
> Proverbs 2:1 (TPT)

Revelation is relational: from Jesus' heart to yours. Pursue what He reveals to you, and you will find the path of your life. Follow the revelation.

Activation

Is there a revelation (a promise, a prophetic word, a great truth in scripture - just anything Jesus showed you) that you want to be real in your life?

1. Write it down. I've lost some very precious words Jesus has given me. I think *I'll never forget this*. But I do. I have a journal for the things Jesus shows me. I treasure them. I reread them months later, and I see patterns and deeper meaning in the fragments Jesus shows me day by day. Many times, they form a big picture that I would never see if I hadn't written the fragments in one place.

2. Ask Jesus to encounter you in that revelation. Ask Him to open it for you. **"Jesus, what does this mean –** for me, make it personal?"

3. **"Jesus, what must I do?"** I want this in my life. I know you reveal things because you want me to experience them. How are you enabling me to do that? What must I do?

Day 21 Jesus Calls, "Your Destiny Begins With Me."

> *There are a thousand hacking at the branches of evil to one who is striking at the root.*
> - Henry David Thoreau

You want to do something significant with your life. You want to somehow change the world, to leave it a little better place because you were here. Most of us do.

Deep in your heart, you believe God has called you to make a difference. And you are the kind of person who does what you know to be right. So, you ask, "Where do I begin?"

Change

Most people begin with a decision. "I am going to change X." It may be a personal change like improving some aspect of your character. Or it may be something you are trying to change on behalf of others: an injustice, a financial need, or healing.

You use self-discipline to try to make this happen. Self-discipline is the approach taken by self-help experts all around the world. People keep creating more books, CDs, apps, and courses to help people change. This $10.8 billion industry is growing rapidly because self-discipline doesn't work. People continue looking for the "new thing," hoping to find real answers.

Change is hard. We are creatures of habit. We don't like change; we fight against it. Recent studies show that human willpower is limited. Like our physical energy, we can exhaust our willpower. When our lives get complicated: we are too busy, too stressed or too tired, we will reach for our willpower, and the cupboard will be empty. Change takes energy: emotional, mental and physical. That's why most New Year's resolutions and diets fail. We don't have the energy to sustain the changes we want to make.

How can we make progress changing the things we most want and need to change?

Begin With a Relationship.

Let's settle this. Without Jesus - nothing.

> "I am the sprouting vine and you're my branches. As you live in union with me as your source, fruitfulness will stream from within you—**but when you live separated from me you are powerless.**
> John 15:5 (TPT)
> "I am the vine; you are the branches. If you remain in me and I in you, you will bear much fruit; **apart from me you can do nothing**.
> John 15:5 (NIV)

With Jesus – everything. It's that simple and that absolute. Your destiny begins with your relationship with Jesus.

> For I can do everything through Christ, who gives me strength.
> Philippians 4:13 (NLT)

Delight

The genuine joy of being with Jesus is the beginning of our journey. It just doesn't make sense to start anywhere else. Your mind would start with its own decisions and disciplines. But destiny is a journey of the heart as well as the mind. **Your heart will take you places your mind can never go.**

> Delight yourself in the Lord; And He will give you the desires of your heart.
>
> Psalm 37:4 (NASB)
>
> Make God the utmost delight and pleasure of your life, and he will provide for you what you desire the most.
>
> Psalm 37:4 (TPT)

You see, God has placed desires in each of our hearts. He made us to be like Him. As His kids, we naturally want what He wants. It's part of our spiritual DNA. Every human being on the planet wants to be loved, accepted, to be significant, etc. But each of us has these desires in different measures. This is part of the one-of-a-kind creation that each of us is.

Desire

No one has your intellect, sense of humor or personality. No one even has the same swirls on the tips of their fingers or ears shaped like yours. And no one comes even close to having the same mix of 20,000 genes that you have. In the same way, no one has the intensity of desires that are part of your spiritual makeup. *Your desires are God's signature written on your heart.*

God created you with desires fully expecting that you would turn to Him to fill them. That's what He delights in as a Father. As you pursue the deepest desires of your heart with God, collaborating together, you make great strides toward your destiny. Destiny is a journey, not a destination. Destiny is being with Jesus, becoming like Jesus, and doing things with Jesus.

As I entered into daily times of delight with God, desires bubbled up inside me – for more of Him, that others would know Him, for justice and righteousness. Some mornings I'm shocked by the intense emotional desire I feel for others. And I realize I am feeling His heart for them. I found that as I enjoyed being with Him, God's desires were becoming my desires.

Decisions.

So, walking together with Jesus, we learn to make good decisions. When we don't know what to do, we ask. Sometimes Jesus tells us and other times He wants us to decide. Yes, He lets us decide a lot of things. Adam named all the animals on the earth. God asked him to. That was a big deal!!

God is such a great Dad! He gives us responsibility as we can handle it. And if we make a mistake, He rescues us. He helps to clean up the mess. And we learn from our mistakes.

Think of a little girl, a toddler, learning to walk. There are so many decisions in just taking a step. Her father shows her and helps her, but lets her decide many things. He lets her take risks. She will fall many times along the way, but in the end, she will be able to walk on her own. And she will know her Dad is there to make sure she won't fall too hard in life. She will also have learned that her Dad trusts her to make decisions and take steps on her own.

Disciplines.

When your desires are at war with your will, who wins? Think dieting. Does willpower win over desires? Not usually and not long term. As we delight in the Lord, He fills our desires. Now willpower and desire can move forward, going in the same direction, arm in arm. No longer foes, desire empowers willpower. And we change.

Destiny. This is life. Being with Jesus. Becoming like Jesus. And doing things with Jesus. Because we are all so different, we will do different things in different ways. But when others look at us, they will say, "I see Jesus in her life."

There are 5 D's in your destiny: Delight, Desire, Decisions, Discipline, and Destiny.

To achieve your destiny, go to the root. Begin with your heart. Genuinely delight in Jesus. Connect your heart to His. Abide - stay there. Let Him fill your desires. You'll be amazed by how tender and thoughtful He is. Now you are ready to make good decisions.

Discipline is an important part of reaching your destiny, but only after you've gone down deep and established your roots – your relationship with Jesus. Most people will see the fruit of your decisions and your discipline. But the strength of your life is your heart rooted firmly in Jesus.

Now go, become awesome, and influence the world. This is your destiny.

Activation

Think about the word "change." What is the first thing about your life that you want to change?

Delight - Ask Jesus to meet you there. Take a few minutes and praise and worship Jesus.

Desire – Tell Jesus what is on your heart, what you want to change?

Jesus, you are my provider. You give me everything I need for life and to be like you. What is your provision for me in this area I want to change?

> He gives us everything we need for life and for holy living. He gives it through His great power. As we come to know Him better, we learn that He called us to share His own shining-greatness and perfect life.
> 2 Peter 1:3 (NLV)

Write down what He tells you.

Decision – What 2 or 3 immediate action steps could you take to cooperate with Jesus in making the change you desire? Write them down. Plan when and where you will do them on a daily basis.

Discipline – Now you are ready to use your willpower. Your heart desire is aligned with your mind decision, Jesus is helping you, and you are actively cooperating with Jesus using self-discipline.

Real change requires repetition for an action to become your default action – what you do without thinking when faced with a situation that requires this response.

This is called "automaticity." Our brains develop routines. These are actual physical pathways in the brain – paths that can be changed.

Much of what we do during the day we don't think about. We just plug in routines and act on them. For example, brushing your teeth, getting undressed, etc. You don't think about these things, you just do them. And we usually do them the same way every day. Automatically. Routinely. That is what you are training your brain to do when you make a change your default response.

Record your daily immediate action steps for several (4-6) weeks until this becomes automatic.

Destiny

There is an old maxim that probably originated from the scripture: "A man reaps what he sows." Galatians 6:7:

> Sow a thought, reap an action;
> sow an action, reap a habit;
> sow a habit, reap a character;
> sow a character, reap a destiny."

The harvest we reap in our lives is the result of the 5 D's: delight, desire, decisions, disciplines, and destiny.

Day 22 Jesus Calls, "Your Weaknesses Don't Disqualify You."

> All God's giants have been weak men who did great things for God because they reckoned on God being with them.
>
> - J. Hudson Taylor

A Man After God's Own Heart

No one loved God more than David. David loved the Bible. He loved everything about God. He was zealous for God's justice. David wrote about being loved by God in the Psalms.

Some decisions define us. David's defining decision was to love God with all he had.

> After removing Saul, he made David their king. God testified concerning him: '**I have found David son of Jesse, a man after my own heart; he will do everything I want him to do**.'
>
> Acts 13:22 (NIV)

I want to be like David: a man after God's own heart, who will do everything God wants me to do. I lived a rough, wild life when I was a young man. My character flaws are many and obvious. My mind wants to disqualify me. But my heart has another cry. I love Jesus. I dream of the day when my life is over, and I go to stand before Him. My heart's desire is to have Jesus say, "Well done, good and faithful servant."

Yeah, I know. People don't talk like that today. But to quote one of my favorite movie characters, Ms. Lina Lamont, "'People? I ain't 'people.'"[14]

David, the shepherd who would become king of Israel, wasn't 'people' either. He was different. He was passionate. He was outrageous – dancing before the Lord and all the people in his underwear. He was lion, bear, and giant-killing brave. David was larger than life.

And so were his character flaws.

Deeply Flawed David

Jessie, David's father, thought so little of young David that when Samuel asked to see all his sons, he didn't bother to call David (1 Samuel 16). That must have hurt.

When David was sent to the battle lines against the Philistines, not to fight, but to bring bread and cheese for his brothers, his brothers were like, "What are you doing here?"

Eliab, David's oldest brother, got particularly nasty, "What are you doing around here anyway?" he demanded. "What about those few sheep you're supposed to be taking care of? I know about your pride and deceit. You just want to see the battle!"

Imagine what their relationship was like after David killed Goliath.

When David should have been out leading his army against the Ammonites, he sent his general instead. David had an affair with Bathsheba, Uriah's wife. Uriah

---

[14] *Singin' in Rain*, dir. Stanley Donen and Gene Kelly, Metro-Goldwyn-Mayer Studios, 1952.

wasn't around. He was fighting the Ammonites for David. She got pregnant. And David had Uriah murdered by sending him to the front of a battle. (2 Samuel 11)

David's family was like a bad soap opera. His son, Amnon, raped his stepsister, Tamar. Absalom killed his stepbrother Amnon because of what he had done. Absalom later rebelled and tried to take David's kingdom (2 Samuel 15-19). And there is more. You get the feeling that David probably wasn't a great dad.

David's redeeming quality was that he genuinely did love God. David's love for God was the defining characteristic of his life. No one else in the Bible is called a man after God's own heart – only David.

David knew he had problems. He knew he didn't have the answers. He asked God to reveal and help him unravel the twisted things in his heart.

> Search me, O God, and know my heart; test me and know my anxious thoughts.
>
> Point out anything in me that offends you, and lead me along the path of everlasting life.
>
> Psalm 139:23-24 (NLT)

And God did search David's heart and lead him in another direction. David had times of sincere repentance. (2 Samuel 12) The changes in his life were real. David also knew that his faults and sins didn't disqualify him. Most of God's heroes of faith had weaknesses and flaws. Big ones! You have flaws too. They do not disqualify you. God made his plan for you knowing all about your flaws.

God's Strength is Greater than Your Weakness

I want to run. I want to run with passion and determination, not distracted, not hobbled or crippled by the decisions of my past or the things that have happened to me. Jesus, set me free to run with You!

> So **search your hearts every day**, my brothers and sisters, and make sure that none of you has **evil or unbelief hiding within you**. For it will lead you astray, and **make you unresponsive to the living God.** This is the time to encourage each other to never be stubborn or hardened by sin's deceitfulness.
>
> Hebrews 3:12-13 (TPT)
>
> So we must **let go of every wound that has pierced us** and the **sin we so easily fall into**. Then we will be able to **run life's marathon race with passion and determination**, for the path has been already marked out before us.
>
> Hebrews 12:1 (TPT)

Like David, God calls us to search our hearts. He will reveal evil and unbelief in our lives. There are other things, things that people have done to us that hurt us deeply – wounds. We need to invite Jesus to bring healing to those wounds.

Read the story of David's life. He went through so much. David overcame everything that had been done to him and his own sin because he loved God. That love compelled him to repent. Sin and unbelief have many effects. Perhaps the worst is they "make you unresponsive to the living God." That is the one thing we need most.

Activation

Pray with me:

Jesus, I love You. I love being loved by You. I love that You have a plan for me. Most of all, I love that you want to be with me. I want to Be With You, I want to Become Like You, and I want to Do everything You have planned for us to do together.

I invite you, Jesus, to search my heart. Show me what needs to be removed. And replace it with more of You. The fruit of your Spirit – Your character. Make me like You.

> *Let us put everything out of our lives that keeps us from doing what we should. Let us keep running in the race that God has planned for us.*
> *Hebrews 12:1 (NLV)*

> *Search me, O God, and know my heart; test me and know my anxious thoughts.*

> *Point out anything in me that offends you, and lead me along the path of everlasting life.*
> *Psalm 139:23-24 (NLT)*

What in me do you want to remove today? Show me. What must I do?

C. Do Things With Jesus

When the Holy Spirit comes to live in us, our lives are no longer about us. The "self-life" is gone. New life has come into us. We live our born-again life in union with Jesus; our lives are His.

> Do you not know that your body is a temple of the Holy Spirit who is within you, whom you have [received as a gift] from God and that **you are not your own [property]**?
>
> You were bought with a price [**you were actually purchased with the precious blood of Jesus and made His own**]. So then, honor and glorify God with your body.
>
> 1 Corinthians 6:19-20 (AMP)

Now, guided and empowered by the same Holy Spirit who raised Jesus from the dead, He begins to change us into the people God dreamed we could be. Part of God's dream for us is what we will do. He has specific works prepared for us to do with Jesus – amazing things.

Jesus surrounds us with people who need Him. And Jesus shows us how to influence our little part of the world. He shows us how to see people, love them and serve them as He does. He asks us to take risks so our faith will grow. He isn't afraid of our failures and mistakes. He knows that rescuing us is one of the ways we will come to trust Him.

As I was writing this, I saw a picture of my Dad, in our garage, working with his father's woodworking tools. My Dad couldn't wait to show us how to use a wood lathe. Some of my fondest memories are working with my Dad on a woodworking project. He loved to teach me things. Father God and Jesus are like that. They want to do things together with us.

Day 23 Jesus Calls, "With Me – Everything. Without Me - Nothing."

> "Yes, I am the vine; you are the branches. Those who remain in me, and I in them, will produce much fruit. For **apart from me you can do nothing.**"
> John 15:5 (NLT)

> "I am the sprouting vine and you're my branches. **As you live in union with me as your source, fruitfulness will stream from within you—but when you live separated from me you are powerless.**"
> John 15:5 (TPT)

Jesus said, "Apart from Me you can do nothing." And He meant it. Without Jesus, we are separated from God, completely at Satan's mercy. Satan has no mercy.

Apostle Paul wrote: "I can do all things through Christ who strengthens me." Philippians 4:13 (NKJV). And he meant it.

Paul knew what he was talking about. When Saul encountered Jesus on the Damascus road, he found out that Jesus was the Messiah. Saul, the persecutor, became Paul, the apostle who took the good news of Jesus to the world and wrote two-thirds of the New Testament. The devil and the Jewish religious leaders went after him with everything they had. In his own words:

> I have worked harder, been put in prison more often, been whipped times without number, and faced death again and again. Five different

times the Jewish leaders gave me thirty-nine lashes. Three times I was beaten with rods. Once I was stoned. Three times I was shipwrecked. Once I spent a whole night and a day adrift at sea. I have traveled on many long journeys. I have faced danger from rivers and from robbers. I have faced danger from my own people, the Jews, as well as from the Gentiles. I have faced danger in the cities, in the deserts, and on the seas. And I have faced danger from men who claim to be believers but are not. I have worked hard and long, enduring many sleepless nights. I have been hungry and thirsty and have often gone without food. I have shivered in the cold, without enough clothing to keep me warm.

2 Corinthians 11:23-27 (NLT)

And yet, toward the end of his life, Paul was able to say:

As for me, my life has already been poured out as an offering to God. The time of my death is near. **I have fought the good fight, I have finished the race, and I have remained faithful**. And now the prize awaits me—the crown of righteousness, which the Lord, the righteous Judge, will give me on the day of his return. And the prize is not just for me but for all who eagerly look forward to his appearing.

2 Timothy 4:6-8 (NLT)

Paul, who didn't become a Christian until later in life,

Paul who had held the cloaks of those who stoned Stephen,

Paul who used prison as an office from which to write Ephesians, Philippians, Colossians, and Philemon,

Paul who was bitten by a deadly poisonous snake and shook it off,

Paul who was harassed, beaten, stoned and left for dead was able to say that he had finished the course God had for his life. He finished and was looking forward to the reward of his faithfulness. I have no doubt that Paul reached the end of his strength so many times that he was used to it. There he learned he could do anything with Jesus. He lived at that place of his weakness/ Jesus' strength.

With Jesus – everything.

Without Jesus – nothing.

Our purpose as born-again sons and daughters of God is to learn to live as Paul did.

Adam and Eve Didn't Last a Day Resisting Satan.

The first time they met the devil, Adam and Eve were persuaded to eat the fruit that cost them their lives. They died spiritually that day. And they gave Satan the authority God had given them to rule the earth for God. Worse, they didn't even know what they had done. That's deception!

Adam and Eve became slaves of Satan by obeying him. Through deception, Satan became ruler of the earth and everyone in it.

> Don't you realize that you become the slave
> of whatever you choose to obey? You can
> be a slave to sin, which leads to death, or

> you can choose to obey God, which leads to
> righteous living.
> Romans 6:16 (NLT)

That vividly describes what happens when we try to live on our own. Satan can be spellbindingly convincing. Remember, this is the guy who convinced one-third of the angels, who lived in the awesome presence of God, to worship him instead of God.

Satan ruled the earth only because there was no man who could resist him.

So, God Sent His Son to Become a Man

God sent Jesus to complete our obedience for us. When Satan murdered the completely innocent Jesus, God pronounced sentence on Satan. The Holy Spirit brought Jesus back to life because there was no death (no disobedience) in Him. Satan's authority over the earth was returned to the man, Jesus. And God ruled that anyone who loves and obeys Jesus will be made righteous by Jesus' perfect performance. Jesus' life is given to them. And His authority is theirs too. They are forever set free from Satan and sin.

Stripped of power, Satan is still the deceiver. He's still dangerous. So, God gave us the Holy Spirit to live in our spirits. He's there to reveal Satan's deceptions and empower us to overcome Satan. The Holy Spirit lives in us to make sure we win this time. The Holy Spirit is our guarantee for all the promises God made to mankind.

God could easily overwhelm us with His presence and power, like Moses on Sinai, trembling in fear; the people, far below, terrified. God doesn't want that. He wants children. He wants to be fatherly toward us. God wants us to grow up in a loving relationship with Him as our Father.

God loves us so we can know what love is. He teaches by demonstration. He disciplines us to stay in the place of love. We learn to respond to Him with love. We learn to love with a love that transforms; it changes us and everyone we touch with His love.

While Adam and Eve couldn't last one day resisting Satan, Jesus perfectly obeyed God his entire life on earth. His obedience completely defeated Satan. Jesus' victory is yours. Don't try to live one day without Jesus.

Begin every day meeting with Jesus. He wants to walk with you.

> Eternal life means to know and experience you as the only true God and to know and experience Jesus Christ, as the Son whom you have sent.
> John 17:3 (TPT)

Activation

Reach out to Jesus with this prayer.

Jesus, I need you. With You, I can do all things because You empower me. Apart from You, I can do nothing. My mind thinks the things I experience on this earth are real. But Your kingdom is more real. And that is where I will spend eternity. Teach me Your ways. Let me see with Your eyes and love with Your heart. I want to be with You, become like You and do everything You have planned for me to do in my time here on earth.

Day 24 Jesus Calls, "Come up Here!"

The Dreaded Phone Call in the Night

Your phone rings in the middle of the night. You fight through the fog of deep sleep, trying to unscramble the voice on the phone.

"This is Memorial General"

"The hospital?"

"Ah, yes. Your father's heart stopped. The doctors got it started again, but you'd better come in." The voice, with calm authority, pronounces judgment, "this may be the end."

"Dad? But how...?"

"That's all I know."

Fear kicks down the door of your heart.

Fear kicks down the door of your heart. You set down your cell phone on the nightstand without ending the call. Your mind begins to race. Your chest tightens, and you start to see yourself standing over your father's grave. Fear and hopelessness tighten their grasp on you. As you scramble around the room looking for your glasses and your clothes, you begin to cry out to God, fervent tearful prayers that die in your throat as hopelessness chokes off your words.

You run to the kitchen and grab your car keys off the hook, then you stop. You remember who God is and who you are.

You remember who God is and who you are.

"Thank you, Father. You love me so much. You look over me and my entire family. You love my father even more than I do."

You walk swiftly to your car.

"God, I can't stay under these circumstances. I can't think to pray. The voices of fear and hopelessness are crushing."

"COME UP HERE." You know that voice. You smile. *Jesus.*

Psalm 100:4 comes to your mind, "Enter his gates with thanksgiving; go into his courts with praise. Give thanks to him and praise his name."

"I praise you, Jesus. You are amazing. I love You so much. I'm so glad You're with me tonight. Thank You. I need You."

You start the car, and as the engine comes to life, you begin to feel the fear lift off of you.

As you drive the dark, empty streets to the hospital, praise rises from your heart. You praise and worship God. You enter His courts with praise. On the corner of Turner and Third Avenue, your car fills with the presence of God. Peace comes into your heart, grabs fear and his crony hopelessness by the scruff of their necks and throws them out. Peace closes the door to your heart and locks it.

Now you're ready to pray.

"Jesus, thank you for inviting me to Your prayer meeting. I submit to You. I draw near to You, Jesus. Devil, I resist you; leave me now.

Jesus, how are You praying for my Dad? What do you want me to know about this situation?"

You wait. When anxious thoughts try to come in you just gently praise them away. When Jesus speaks, it may be a picture in your mind, a still small voice, a Scripture or an inner knowing that you recognize as Him. You wait, confident Jesus will answer. You've done this before – many times.

You have the faintest impression – a picture of a heart beating. And a wave of peace washes over you. You have His answer.

You pull into the hospital parking lot and park your car. Now, you pray. You pray with great faith and calm authority. You declare life over your Father. You pray for wisdom for all the doctors and nurses. You thank Jesus and Father God.

You now enter the hospital prepared to change the atmosphere and bring the full kingdom of God to bear in this situation. Your spirit is seated with Jesus in heaven. That's where you are praying from.

Come Up Here?

Our physical life is limited to the earth. But we are spirits. We live in a body, and we have a soul, but we are spirits. When we were born again, "God raised us up with Christ and seated us with him in the heavenly realms in Christ Jesus...."

> But because of his great love for us, God, who
> is rich in mercy, made us alive with Christ even
> when we were dead in transgressions—it is by
> grace you have been saved. **And God raised us
> up with Christ and seated us with him in the
> heavenly realms in Christ Jesus**,
>
> Ephesians 2:4-6 (NIV)

Jesus is seated in the throne room of God, at God's right hand. This is the throne of grace and mercy where we can go to get help. (Hebrews 4:16) We enter the outer gates by giving thanks. We enter God's courts, His presence, with praise.

Paul talked about three heavens (2 Corinthians 12). The first is the earth and the atmosphere above us. The second heaven is where demonic powers and principalities control the earth from. People without Jesus live their lives UNDER the principalities and powers of darkness – under the problems, fears, and darkness covering this world. The third heaven, high above the other two, is where Jesus is, high above any principality or power. Jesus is seated on his throne at the right hand of God.

When we pray, we go to Jesus – boldly approaching His throne of grace and mercy. What is Jesus doing in heaven? He's interceding for us.

> Therefore he is able, once and forever, to save
> those who come to God through him. **He lives
> forever to intercede with God on their behalf.**
>
> Hebrews 7:25 (NLT)

Now, I don't know about you, but when I join Jesus' prayer meeting, I don't want to lead. I listen. How are you praying, Jesus? What is Your provision in this?

When He answers, then I know how to pray. I'm not praying to Him; I'm praying to God with Jesus. And I KNOW that prayer will be answered.

Activation

It's easy to live life under situations – overwhelmed and overcome. You weren't meant to live under the devil's thumb or your neighbor's either for that matter. Learn to "come up here" to where Jesus is. Everything looks different when you rise above the problems of life. 2 Corinthians 4-6.

Think of a situation or problem that is weighing you down, stressing you out. Follow the path above.

1. Rise above your situation by heartfelt thanksgiving and praise. Psalm 100:4 (above)

2. Praise and worship until you feel the peace of drawing near to God. Submit to God. (It's not what "I" want. I submit to You, Lord), draw near to God and resist the devil (I resist your thoughts, emotions, and influence).

> Therefore submit to God. Resist the
> devil and he will flee from you. Draw
> near to God and He will draw near to
> you. Cleanse *your* hands, *you* sinners;
> and purify *your* hearts, *you* double-minded.
> James 4:7-8 (NKJV)

3. Join Jesus' prayer meeting. Ephesians 2:6 (above), Hebrews 7:25 (above)

Sometimes, how we see a person or situation is the problem.

Jesus, show me how you see _____ (a person, situation or problem). Let Jesus show you His perspective. That may be all you need.

How are you praying, Jesus? What is Your provision for me in this?

Approach Jesus knowing there is always an answer. (2 Peter 1:3-5 (below) and Philippians 4:19 (below).

Faith-Building Scriptures for Praying With Jesus

Let us then approach God's throne of grace with confidence, so that we may receive mercy and find grace to help us in our time of need.

Hebrews 4:16 (NIV)

This is the confidence we have in approaching God: that if we ask anything according to his will, he hears us. And if we know that he hears us—whatever we ask—we know that we have what we asked of him.

1 John 5:14-15 (NIV)

And my God will liberally supply (fill until full) your every need according to His riches in glory in Christ Jesus.

Philippians 4:19 (AMP)

By his divine power, God has given us everything we need for living a godly life. We have received all of this by coming to know him, the one who called us to himself by means of his marvelous glory and excellence. And because of his glory and excellence, he has given us great and precious promises. These are the promises that enable you to share his divine nature and escape the world's corruption caused by human desires.

2 Peter 1:3-4 (NLT)

Day 25 Jesus calls, "Give, and it will be given to you."

> If you go looking for a friend, you'll find that friends are very scarce. If you go out to be a friend, you'll find them everywhere.
> - Zig Ziglar

I like this quote because it is intuitively true, but at the same time, it is insightful. Most of us aren't very self-aware. We judge others by their actions. We judge ourselves by our intentions. This simple thought about finding friends is based on a deep truth that will prove true in every area of your life.

> "Give, and it will be given to you. They will pour into your lap a good measure—pressed down, shaken together, and running over [with no space left for more]. For **with the standard of measurement you use [when you do good to others], it will be measured to you in return**."

> Luke 6:38 (AMP)

Want love? Give love.

Want kindness? Be kind.

Want to be heard? Listen.

Want to be forgiven? Forgive others and forgive yourself.

Want to not be judged? Don't judge others.

Give and it will be given to you.

In 1997, Karen, my wife, and I moved from a small town in Pennsylvania to Hong Kong. We gave our car away. We gave away all our furniture to friends and family. Shortly after arriving in Hong Kong we found an apartment. My wife's friend was moving into a new apartment and bought all new furniture. She gave us a whole household of furniture. Beautiful furniture. Then people gave us cars. We gave away a Chrysler. Over the twelve years we lived in Hong Kong we were given a Toyota Camry and two BMW's. Awesome cars! A few years later a family member gave us all their furniture when they moved back to the U.S.

We didn't pray for any of this to happen. And we were surprised each time it did. God just gave us gift after gift. With every gift, He reminded us of His love and faithfulness to us. While in Hong Kong we had some tough years financially. God's gifts touched us deeply. And He taught us about giving and receiving from the heart.

Giving in Relationships

My wife, Karen, is an amazing person. She has taught me so much about life and love. She's also smarter than me. English is her fourth language. We speak in English because my Cantonese is embarrassingly bad.

From time to time we have disagreements. I think fast and overreact. For ten years, I was an alcoholic. No one is more self-centered than alcoholics and drug addicts. When I became a Christian (a year before I first met Karen), I broke free from alcohol. It took a lot longer to deal with the ravages of alcohol on my personality.

In the early years of our marriage, we had more than a few misunderstandings. My rocket of rage would go up. And Karen would shrink back from my anger. She would get quiet. I would come down quickly, apologize (I wasn't a complete jerk), and try to talk through what just happened. Karen would sit there looking hurt, refuse to look at me, and just be quiet. I would talk and talk, thinking that would help. Then, she would say a few words and I would get offended and go off again. After a while, she didn't want to talk at all when I got upset. "It will only make it worse."

She was right and I was thoroughly ashamed of myself. I prayed and prayed. I begged God to take away the anger. Over time, He did. But we still had disagreements. And I began to ask Karen why she would simply close down when we had cross words. It took me a ridiculously long time to realize that she became bottled up with emotion. It is tough to express emotions in another language. I knew that from experience. If I wanted to help her, I had to give her permission to talk.

I had to honor and respect her enough to wait, to not interrupt, and to let her say things I didn't want to hear. When I began to give Karen the love and respect she deserved, I set her free to talk. It's still hard for me to wait, but love waits. The gift of Karen's wisdom and our mutual understanding is the reward. I'm still impulsive. She is still a voice of wisdom in my ear and the love of my life. She loves me with a love that defies description. *Give and it will be given to you, pressed down, shaken together and running over.*

This works in All relationships.

With Jesus.

190

Want to hear God? Listen.

> "Be still, and know that I am God!"
> Psalm 46:10 (NLT)
> "My sheep listen to my voice; I know them, and
> they follow me."
> John 10:27 (NLT)

Want to be closer to Jesus?

What does scripture say about getting close to Jesus?

> **Move your heart closer and closer to God, and
> he will come even closer to you**. But make sure
> you cleanse your life, you sinners, and keep your
> heart pure and stop doubting.
> James 4:8 (TPT)

Can you see it? You step out toward God, and He comes
running to you.

> So he got up and went to his father. But while
> he was still a long way off, his father saw him
> and was filled with compassion for him; he
> ran to his son, threw his arms around him
> and kissed him.
>
> Luke 11:20 (NIV) (Jesus telling the parable of the
> prodigal son)

Do it! And be amazed. Turn your heart to Jesus. Step out
toward Him. And He will come running to you.

Want to do great things for God?

Develop the habit of immediate obedience. God
rewards our gift of obedience with awesome

assignments. I can't count the times when I showed up at my usual prayer time tired, stressed or in pain. I'm there to obey God's command to pray. Praying was the last thing I wanted to do. Those are the evenings when I receive very specific prayer assignments. God leads me to pray for particular people or situations and I've seen those prayers answered in amazing ways. Give faithfulness and receive awesome things from God because you showed up when it wasn't easy.

Want to lead?

Serve. In God's kingdom, leaders are servants.

> But this is not your calling. You will lead by a different model. The greatest one among you will live as one called to serve others without honor. The greatest honor and authority is reserved for the one who has a servant heart.
> Luke 22:26 (TPT)

Want help?

Help someone.

Want people to care about you?

Care about someone?

Want faith?

Faith requires an action. Take a risk.

> He called out to them, "Friends, haven't you any fish?"
> "No," they answered.
> He said, "Throw your net on the right side of the boat and you will find some." When they did,

they were unable to haul the net in because of
the large number of fish.
John 21:5-6 (NIV)

Foundation

God has given you everything you need for life and
godliness by your knowledge of Him and coming to
know Him. Step closer to Him and He will fill your
deepest desires and needs.

> Jesus has the power of God. And his power
> has given us everything we need to live a life
> devoted to God. We have these things because
> we know him. Jesus chose us by his glory
> and goodness....
> 2 Peter 1:3 (ERV)

Give time, effort, thought, energy and heart to
Jesus and you will be overwhelmed by His response.
I promise! Millions have experienced this and
you will too.

Activation

*Lord, from the depths of my soul, I want to be a giver.
What gift could I give you today, Jesus? What do you
most want from me?*

*Listen. Then wholeheartedly give. Take immediate, small
steps to give Jesus what He most wants from you. There
is such joy in giving.*

Day 26 Jesus calls, "This is How You Overcome: by Character."

> Do not be overcome by evil, but overcome
> evil with good.
> Romans 12:21 (NIV)

Jesus warned us we would have trouble in this world. And we will. It's important to know how to overcome.

1. We overcome by faith which brings God's power to change whatever comes against us. Faith grows best in the soil of adversity.

2. And we overcome by God empowering us to outgrow (to grow stronger in character than) the adversity we face. The person or problem still exists, but we become strong enough that the adversity no longer affects us. We have outgrown it. Jesus loves to teach us how to live in His character so we can bring healing to the character of others.

The Holy Spirit who lives in you isn't a baby Holy Spirit who grows only as you do. Oh, no! All the power of God's love, joy, peace, patience, kindness, goodness, gentleness, and self-control – the fruit of God's character, dwells in you. Let me say this again: **the complete fullness of God's character (the fruit of the Holy Spirit) is available to you, NOW**. The Holy Spirit, who lives in you, has it. Learn how to receive His character and live from it, instead of staggering and stumbling through life in your flawed character.

> But **the Holy Spirit produces this kind of fruit in our lives: love, joy, peace, patience, kindness,**

goodness, faithfulness, gentleness, and self-control. There is no law against these things!

Those who belong to Christ Jesus have nailed the passions and desires of their sinful nature to his cross and crucified them there. Since **we are living by the Spirit**, let us follow the Spirit's leading in every part of our lives.

Galatians 5:22, 25 (NLT)

Let's see what this would look like.

The Angry Boss

Steve stumbled out of the conference room. Another bombastic team meeting. He went back to his office, gently closed the door, slipped into his chair, and collapsed on his desk, his head in his hands. *I can't do this anymore.* Steve had left Stroogle to join Frank's startup. They had been friends in high school. Frank was the most brilliant guy he knew. But as a leader, Frank was a train wreck.

Steve began to talk to Jesus. He'd been doing that a lot lately. "Frank is destroying us. He's so angry. No. Worse – he's abusive. I can't work like this."

Jesus answered, "I'm glad you agree."

Steve was relieved. "I'm going to leave. I can work anywhere." A huge weight lifted off of Steve's shoulders when he thought about leaving.

"Steve, I gave you this job."

"Yes, Lord. I know you did. But you agree. I can't go on... I don't understand."

"Steve, Frank is one of mine."

"He's a Christian? You gotta be kidding!"

"Not yet, but soon. His childhood was a nightmare. He's come a long way."

"Okay. I'll pray for Him. So, where should I apply?"

"Right here."

"Huh!"

"This job isn't your assignment. Frank is."

"But Jesus…"

"Steve, I sent people for you."

Steve saw the faces of friends and the things they had done to help him when his life was an alcoholic mess. He remembered wondering why Bill wasn't offended like everyone else. Steve had been a mean drunk. Bill had just shown up in his life and wouldn't go away, no matter what Steve did to him. As he thought of Bill, Steve nodded.

"Okay. I'll stay. But I don't know how to help him?"

"Give him what he lacks."

Steve saw a picture of several golden bowls in heaven and each was filled. The golden bowls were overflowing, falling to the earth like rain. He saw people covered in darkness, deep darkness. Sad people. Angry people. People in pain. As the rain hit those people, their lives became lighter. The rain changed their pain, over time, to peace. Then joy.

Steve looked closer at each golden bowl. He could feel the contents of each: love, faith, hope, joy, peace, patience, kindness, goodness, faithfulness, gentleness, and self-control. He knew these were God's character. The fruit of the Holy Spirit. Galatians 5.

The picture was interrupted by an angry voice. "What's wrong with you? Are you really that stupid?" Frank was screaming at Steve's team again.

The team sat at their cubicles, their heads down, but their body language was clear. Resentment. Burning anger.

Steve rushed out, "Hi boss." Steve smiled.

Frank stopped, turned. "Have you seen this?" He threw the stack of papers in his hand in the air.

"Come, tell me what's wrong. I'll fix it." Steve motioned to his office.

Frank went in, slammed the door and continued his rant. Steve's team could hear every word through the closed door. That became a regular scene in the office. Frank vented his rage on Steve for weeks.

"Steve has the patience of Job," they said.

No, Steve had the patience of God. Over time, Frank ran out of rage. He poured it out. Steve's response was patience, intelligent listening, real answers and love that left Frank shaking his head. Steve learned to live in God's love for Frank. Frank's anger didn't hurt Steve. God protected Steve's heart. Frank began to change. Slowly. Then suddenly. Jesus' words to Steve came to pass. "Frank is one of Mine."

This is a parable. But it is true. I've seen my wife, Karen, change people by loving them with God's love. God has given her this gift of seeing people as they could be, not as they are. And she treats them as the person God is transforming them into. It's a powerful thing. I know. She did it to me.

Give people the character trait they lack.

Sow patience in people's lives.

Sow love. Most people don't love well because they have been poorly loved. We can't give what we've never received. That's why the Holy Spirit is in us, working the character of Christ in us.

The fruit of the Holy Spirit are powerful weapons. Hate the behavior, but love the people. This is how we overcome: we fill the world with God's character by giving it to them.

Ask Jesus what a person needs in a specific situation. Reach out and take it from the well of the Holy Spirit and give it to that person. Overcoming evil is not just beating it back and winning a battle. If the darkness is still in that person, it will find another reason to come out and fight. Overcome by God's faith and God's character. God will give them to you for each situation you seek.

When Jesus shows you what a person needs, you can be confident that what you are giving them will have an impact. Maybe not today or tomorrow, but soon and powerfully. And you can boldly pray for their heart to be changed. You will be bold because Jesus showed you what they need.

God's way of changing us – all of us, is replacement.

So, I say, let the Holy Spirit guide your lives. Then you won't be doing what your sinful nature craves. The sinful nature wants to do evil, which is just the opposite of what the Spirit wants. And **the Spirit gives us desires that are the opposite of what the sinful nature desires**. These two forces are constantly fighting each other, so you are not free to carry out your good intentions.

The Holy Spirit produces this kind of fruit in our lives: love, joy, peace, patience, kindness, goodness, faithfulness, gentleness, and self-control. ...

[25] Since we are living by the Spirit, **let us follow the Spirit's leading in every part of our lives**. [26] Let us not become conceited, or provoke one another, or be jealous of one another.

Galatians 5:16-17, 22-26 (NLT)

Activation

"Jesus, who can I influence today with Your character - your loving nature?"

"Show me the experience they need to be healed."

Now, go practice giving people God's character. This is how we overcome. When people hit us with evil, we turn it into good. We overcome their evil with God's goodness. Be patient with people who no one listens to and see how they respond. Rude people wilt under kindness. And here is maybe the best part. As you learn to receive God's character to give it to others, His character will become yours and theirs.

Day 27 Jesus Calls, "This is How You Overcome: by Faith."

> For everyone born of God overcomes the world. This is the victory that has overcome the world, even our faith.
> 1 John 5:4 (NIV)

Faith is a gift from God.

> For by grace you have been saved through faith; and that not of yourselves, it is the gift of God; not as a result of works, so that no one may boast.
> Ephesians 2:8-9 (NASB)

...God has allotted to each a measure of faith.

Romans 12:3 (NASB)

Jesus initiates and completes/perfects our faith.

> We look away from the natural realm and we fasten our gaze onto Jesus who birthed faith within us and who leads us forward into faith's perfection.
> Hebrews 12:2 (TPT)

Our faith can fail.

Jesus prayed that Peter's faith wouldn't fail, even as he sinned by denying Christ. And it didn't. We can pray this prayer for ourselves and others.

> "But I have pleaded in prayer for you, Simon, that your faith should not fail. So when you

have repented and turned to me again,
strengthen your brothers."
Luke 22:32 (NLT)

Our faith can grow.

> In 2 Corinthians 10: 15 (CEV), Paul says, "But
> I hope that **as you become stronger in your
> faith**, we will be able to reach many more of the
> people around you."

As we grow in relationship with Jesus, we increase
our faith. We do that by having adventures with God.
Taking risks. Through faith we overcome, we have
breakthroughs. These are battles fought and won. But
what if I fail? At one point I was trying so hard to "get it
right" that I didn't want to step out in faith. I held back.
I missed some opportunities to do some good things
because I was afraid. Let me encourage you. God isn't
upset with people who "miss it." He is proud of you.
"Look at the lion heart of my son. Once he learns to
hear my voice, what a warrior he will become."

Every faith adventure begins with hearing Jesus.

> "So faith *comes* from hearing, and hearing by
> the word (rhema – the spoken word) of Christ."
> Romans 10:17 (NASB). (parenthesis added
> for clarity).

Jesus teaches us to know his voice. When we know it
is Jesus speaking to us, we have faith to do what He
shows us to do.

Faith involves risk.

Faith is having an inner knowing and stepping out to take a risk. Faith is bringing spiritual things we can't see into the physical world that we can see. Sometimes, it's a huge risk! When you step out in faith, you are stepping out in reliance on God because you know this thing is too big, too impossible for you, but somehow you believe God is in it, so you are saying, "Yes, Lord."

Those who hold back, afraid to take a risk - refusing to depend on God - to put their lives in God's hands, are actually saying, "No."

They are the Israelites who saw amazing miracles in Egypt - water turned to blood, the firstborn of all Egypt dying, but their children saved by the blood of the lamb put on their doorposts. They saw a pillar of cloud leading them every day and a pillar of fire every night for forty years. They saw quail fall from the heavens when they demanded food and water gushing from a rock when they demanded water. Every morning they collected the bread of God which fell from heaven like the dew - manna. Still, they grumbled, worried and complained, refusing to trust God.

> The same people who were delivered from
> bondage and brought out of Egypt by Moses
> were the ones who heard and still rebelled.
> ...They grieved God for forty years by sinning
> in their unbelief, until they dropped dead
> in the desert.
> Hebrews 3:16, 18 (TPT)

They were unable to receive their inheritance, because of their unbelief and unwillingness to trust God.

> So we see that they were not able to enter
> [into His rest—the promised land] because of
> unbelief *and* an unwillingness to trust in God.
> Hebrews 3:19 (AMP)

God is not pleased with those who shrink back.

> And he also says, "My righteous ones will live
> from my faith. But if fear holds them back, my
> soul is not content with them!"
> Hebrews 10:38 (TPT)

> Take care, brothers and sisters, that there not
> be in any one of you a wicked, unbelieving heart
> [which refuses to trust and rely on the Lord, a
> heart] that turns away from the living God.
> Hebrews 3:12 (AMP)

**God uses difficult times to grow both faith and
character to overcome.**

> My fellow believers, when it seems as though
> you are facing nothing but difficulties see it as
> an invaluable opportunity to experience the
> greatest joy that you can! **For you know that
> when your faith is tested, it stirs up power
> within you to endure all things.** And **then
> as your endurance grows even stronger, it
> will release perfection into every part of
> your being until there is nothing missing and
> nothing lacking.**
> James 1:2-4 (TPT)

Why should we have joy in difficulties? Because we are
developing faith muscle and at the same time the Holy
Spirit is strengthening our character, providing what
we lack so we can stand strong until we win. God's

character formed in us enables us to endure all things, standing strong in our belief that God is faithful. Faith.

Faith is not optional.

Faith is what reaches into heaven and brings the things of God to earth. God has amazing things for you, beginning with eternal life with Him. But you have to believe Him - trust Him, to receive them.

> And without faith it is impossible to please God, because anyone who comes to him must believe that he exists and that he rewards those who earnestly seek him.
> Hebrews 11:6 (NIV)

Activation

I don't want to get mechanical here and tell you the five laws or anything like that. Faith is relational. It's us being touched by Jesus, hearing Him, then walking in what He said. But faith can be built up; we can grow stronger in faith.

Years ago, I read a book about faith where the author said to grow your faith by trusting God for something you need today. For example, if you need lunch money, don't bring it. And ask God to take you to lunch.

God knows you aren't testing Him (scripture tells us not to). You are developing stronger faith.

Ask Jesus to help you grow in faith. Like muscles, faith grows when exercised. It's important to learn a lifestyle of faith – a lifestyle of taking risks. Over time, you will learn that what Jesus tells you is more real than what you see in this world. Rock solid faith comes from experiencing Jesus' goodness again and again.

Jesus, today I will need _____ (be specific). I'm going to leave my _____ at home. I'm asking you to provide that for me today. Again, I'm not testing You. I know You give me everything I need for life and to be like You. Today, I am taking a risk, to make my faith grow.

> By his divine power, God has given us everything we need for living a godly life. We have received all of this by coming to know him...
>
> 2 Peter 1:3 (NLT)

My Story

I was teaching at Slippery Rock University of Pennsylvania when I read about this faith-building exercise. I decided to intentionally build my faith. I had three classes that day, and I needed a pen to take attendance in each class and make notes about how much we covered in each class. I intentionally left all my pens at home.

I rejoiced during my 45-minute drive to the university. I got out of my car and walked to my building, my eyes glued to the ground, looking for a pen. I got to my office, no pen. I walked the hall, looking at the floor the whole way to my classroom. No pen. I was getting nervous. The previous class was leaving as I walked into the classroom. My students began to arrive. And there, in the back of the classroom, on the floor was this old, beat up, none too clean pen. I wiped it off and used it all day. My faith soared.

I've taken some big risks. In 1989, I got on a plane to China with $25.75 in my pocket. I was going there to teach for a year. I was in Los Angeles completing training when I ran out of money. I felt the Lord told me it was okay not to ask family or friends for money before my flight left Los Angeles. He wanted me to trust Him as I began my adventure of teaching in China.

The officials from my university who were supposed to meet me at the Shanghai airport with a ticket to Guangzhou never showed up. I was stuck in Shanghai, over 750 miles from the university I was going to teach at in Guangzhou. And I didn't yet speak the language. God gave me a place to stay that night, an airline ticket to my destination city, and a month's pay in advance when I arrived at my university.

I've also taken great risks that God was not in. Those were painful times. But God rescued me. I actually believe my faith grew more by being rescued than at other times. And I learned humility, a key life skill for anyone who walks with Jesus.

God is faithful; it's who He is. He cannot be anything but faithful. I still struggle to have faith for specific things from time to time, but now I realize that my faith is not in what God is going to do as much as it is in who He is. My faith is in God's goodness.

> Faith is deliberate confidence in the character
> of God whose ways you may not understand
> at the time.
> - Oswald Chambers

Faith is too important to neglect. Don't wait until you face a crisis to try your faith. Great faith grows from small risks. Develop a lifestyle of risk-taking for Jesus, and one day you will wake up with great faith.

> For everyone who has been born of God overcomes the world. And this is the victory that has overcome the world—our faith.

> 1 John 5:4 (ESV)

Day 28 Jesus Calls, "I Will Rescue You."

> "Even to your old age and gray hairs I am he, I
> am he who will sustain you. I have made you
> and I will carry you; I will sustain you and **I will
> rescue you**."
> Isaiah 46:4 (NIV)

My Rescue

It had been a brutal trip, over 30 hours in a van
crammed with research, luggage, a debate coach
and five fellow university debaters. We arrived in
Morgantown, West Virginia at night. I was staggering
with exhaustion when I got out of the van. But my car
wasn't there.

We had just spent an intense week in a debate
workshop at the University of Arizona, not to mention
the 4,200 miles and six days spent in that van, three
days down, three days back and broken air conditioning
part of the way. It was August 1979. I was a 23, fresh out
of the Air Force and a sophomore at WVU. I went to a
friend's house and called long distance. (There were no
cell phones back then.) My girlfriend wasn't answering
my calls. She hadn't been for days.

I was 150 miles from home and wouldn't have access to
my apartment in Morgantown for another two weeks
– when university started. I had been living on my own
since I joined the Air Force five years earlier. But I didn't
have a choice. I made the call.

My stepfather, C.R., answered. I told him I was stuck in
Morgantown and Zelda (not her real name) had my car.
I didn't know where she was. She was probably there, in

my hometown. He said, "Oh. Okay. Your Mom and I will drive down. She doesn't get home until eleven tonight, so we'll see you around two." And that was that.

They arrived at two o'clock in the morning, we exchanged hugs, and I got in the car, fully expecting a lecture. It was humiliating to have to be rescued by your parents when you're 23 and have been on your own for over five years. They began with small talk. I waited.

Then a question. "What happened to Zelda?"

Okay, here we go.

I explained she became more distant as we talked during the two weeks I was gone. We all knew she was at a tough place in her life. And in the last few days, I realized Zelda and I seemed to be going different directions.

Forty years later, I still remember the moon that night. I kept looking out the car window, at the moon. I was reluctant to look at Mom and C.R., afraid to hear what they would say. They had reservations about Zelda. I knew that. They were right. Now, I knew that too.

C.R. cleared his throat. *Here it comes*, I thought.

He said, "Dave, it's going to take a very special girl to be with you. You have dreams, and you're going after them. Not everyone does that."

I sat there, tears coming to my eyes. And that was it. That's all they said.

C.R. drove six hours that night and, as I remember, had to work early the next day. He never mentioned it. I felt so loved as I sat in their car watching the moonlight on the mountains, not bothering to wipe the tears from my cheeks. That was one of the best rides of my life.

That's how God rescues me. And He's had to do it more than a few times. He goes to great lengths to come to me, wherever I am, and He brings me home with love. Somehow, being rescued by God makes me trust Him even more than when I fight faith battles and win. I guess it's knowing that no matter if I fail or succeed, He's always there for me.

God will rescue us. Even in our foolishness.

Our faith in God grows because He is our Deliverer. God rescued me from alcoholism when I was 32 and forever gained my trust. Being rescued is convincing proof that God's love and power are personal – they are for you, for me.

Several other translations of Isaiah 46:4 say "save" instead of "rescue." E.g.

> I will be your God throughout your lifetime—
> until your hair is white with age. I made you,
> and I will care for you. **I will** carry you along
> and **save you**.
> Isaiah 46:4 (NLT)

Jesus came to save us. The Greek word sozo, used over 100 times in the New Testament, means **"to save, to heal, to deliver."** Strong's Exhaustive Concordance, Greek 4982. Sózó.[15]

---

[15] Strong's Exhaustive Concordance: New American Standard Bible. Updated ed. La Habra: Lockman Foundation, 1995. http://www.biblestudytools.com/concordances/strongs-exhaustive-concordance/.

Sozo means to save from sin.

> For the Son of Man came to seek and save those
> who are lost.
> Luke 19:10 (NLT)
>
> If you declare with your mouth, "Jesus is Lord,"
> and believe in your heart that God raised him
> from the dead, you will be saved.
> Romans 10:9 (NIV)

Sozo means to save from sickness and disease.

> Jesus turned and saw her. "Take heart,
> daughter," he said, "your faith has healed you."
> And the woman was healed at that moment.
> Matthew 9:22 (NIV)
>
> And Jesus said to him, "Go, for your faith has
> healed you." Instantly the man could see, and
> he followed Jesus down the road.
> Mark 10:52 (NLT)

Sozo means to save from Satan and demons

> Then those who had seen what happened told
> the others how the demon-possessed man had
> been healed.
> Luke 8:36 (NLT)

God's plan is to rescue you. No matter what. He sent
Jesus to make a way, and He is working to save you
and I today.

And He will do it with great joy and love. He's not
reluctant. And He's not angry about it. He hates sin,
but He loves you. And like any good father, He will

protect you and help you even when you created your own mess.

> ... for He has said,
> "I will never [under any
> circumstances] desert you
> [nor give you up nor leave you without support,
> nor will I in any degree leave you helpless],
> nor will I forsake or let you down
> or relax My hold on you [assuredly not]!"
> So we take comfort and are encouraged and confidently say,
> "The Lord is my Helper [in time of need], I will not be afraid.
> What will man do to me?"
> Hebrews 13:5-6 (AMP)

God can build your faith - by victories or by rescuing you.

When your heart is for God, and you take a risk, God WILL build your faith. You will receive what you prayed for, or you will fail spectacularly and God will rescue you. Either way, you will know God loves you and is there for you. I have a few spectacular failures in my past. I know how faith-building it is to be rescued and restored by God.

What God can't bless is when we hold back, refusing to believe or trust. At those times we choose fear over faith. We are following Satan, not God.

> And, "But my righteous one will live by faith. And **I take no pleasure in the one who shrinks back."** But we do not belong to those who

shrink back and are destroyed, but to those who have faith and are saved.

Hebrews 10:38-39 (NIV)

Here is God's remedy for fear: submit to God, draw near to Him, and He will come close to you, then resist the devil and the devil will flee from you because God is with you. It's like rushing home after school to get your big brother and go find the kid that is bullying you. Jesus is our big brother.

> Therefore submit to God. Resist the devil and he will flee from you. Draw near to God and He will draw near to you. Cleanse your hands, you sinners; and purify your hearts, you double-minded.
>
> James 4:7-8 (NKJV)
>
> For God has not given us a spirit of fear and timidity, but of power, love, and self-discipline.
>
> 2 Timothy 1:7 (NLT)

Activation

1. What have you been holding back on? What do you feel God wants you to do, but you haven't done it because it's too risky?

2. Recommit your desires to God. Submit to God's will. Ask Him to confirm what you thought you heard.

3. Then step out in faith. Take the first step toward that goal and see if a bridge appears beneath your feet. Succeed or fail, your faith will grow because God will rescue you.

Day 29 Jesus Calls, "Be a Blessing to Someone Today."

> Lord make me a blessing to someone today.
> - Jan Karon

Jesus lived an interruptible life.

As you read through the four gospel accounts of Jesus' life, one thing becomes clear: Jesus was interruptible.

God showed Jesus who to talk to and who to pray for. Jesus lived His whole life in response to Father God. Jesus had plans, but He was always ready to stop and help someone.

This lifestyle is the privilege of our life with Christ. Jesus walked the earth as a man with the authority of God. He encountered darkness and released the authority God gave Him to overcome it. Jesus invites us to live with Him, a life interrupted by opportunities to touch specific people around us with Jesus' authority, His love, and His power.

> God has made us what we are. In Christ Jesus, God made us new people so that we would spend our lives doing the good things he had already planned for us to do.
> Ephesians 2:10 (ERV)

A Person You Normally Wouldn't Notice

I felt the Lord pointing her out while standing in her checkout line at Publix. She was the kind of person we usually don't notice – middle-aged, average height, normal weight, average looking, with no distinguishing features. Why was Jesus pointing her out to me? I looked past the customers in front of me and saw that she was wearing a brace on her left wrist. As she picked up a heavy item to scan it, I saw her wince. She was in pain. Yet she smiled at everyone and was quite friendly.

Under my breath, I asked, "Jesus, what do you want me to do?"

I didn't hear any instructions from Jesus. He prompted me to notice her and left the rest to me. There was no one behind me in the checkout line. That would help. Too soon, it was my turn to check out. Now, I was nervous. *You are going to make a fool of yourself.* I tried to ignore the voice of fear.

"Hi, how are you?"

She smiled. "Fine. And you?" I could see the pain on her face as she scanned some of the heavier items from my cart.

"What happened to your arm?" I pointed to the brace.

She frowned. "Carpal tunnel. I got it from this." She scanned an item.

I listened. She told me she was in pain every day and her wrist wouldn't heal unless she stopped using it so much. She had to work and didn't have a choice. I had a strong impression that she was the only support for her family from the way she talked.

I couldn't believe what came out of my mouth. "Jesus will heal you. I want to pray for your arm."

She said, "I think I'm going to cry."

I prayed a jumbled prayer. I didn't do this boldly. I stumbled and bumbled and was surprised at what I was saying even as I said it. But I felt the love of Jesus reaching out and touching that woman. I felt Jesus' love drawing her to Him.

Someone stepped up behind me and began putting groceries on the conveyor belt. I asked her how her wrist felt. She said it was better but still hurt.

I should have prayed again. But I was reluctant to keep the person behind me waiting. She thanked me, and I left. I apologized to Jesus for not being bolder. Despite my timidity, that woman, whose name I still don't know was deeply moved as Jesus touched her. I looked for her every time I went in that store but never saw her again.

This story is from my journal for March 15, 2014. Through this and similar experiences I've learned that if we are willing to take risks and, like Paul, be a "fool" for Jesus, He will give us precious opportunities to touch people with His love. And we become bolder with practice.

If you immediately obey, you will have amazing adventures with Jesus. Lives will be changed: theirs and yours.

A Power Encounter

The sunrise was glorious that morning, a ball of fire rising from the ocean, growing larger, brighter. Soon the reds and oranges were replaced with intense yellow-white light. Another day had begun at the Pompano Beach Café. Karen, my wife, and I were their first customers. Not too many tourists begin their day at 6:30. We weren't tourists. We lived nearby, and this was our favorite thing to do. Each sunrise was an original work of art, always different, and always inspiring.

We sat in the café, watching the waves shimmering in the early morning light. Our waitress was new that day. I thought she was Chinese at first glance, but no. We always talk to the Chinese people we meet because Karen is from Hong Kong. Her name was Shani. She was an American Indian. And she had just come to Pompano Beach from Chicago. As she brought our breakfast, we talked some more. She was struggling with some big life decisions. She came to southern Florida to get away and think about her life. We talked for a long time. We were still the only customers in the café.

"Shani, we're Christians. I'd like to pray for you, to ask God to help you with what you're going through."

She smiled sweetly. She told us she was a spiritual person and said something about crystals. I had discerned some new age influence earlier. She wanted me to pray for her.

I lightly touched her arm as I began to pray for her. I was going to ask God to give her wisdom and help her with the problems she had shared with us. I don't remember what I said. But when I began, wham! The power of God hit Shani, she staggered and stepped back from our table to regain her balance. I felt it too.

Shani was surprised, but not afraid. She said something like, "That was so powerful. So pure. I feel such peace." She told us she had felt spiritual power before, but never like that. Nothing like that! She kept saying how wonderful that touch made her feel. She felt peace – deep peace about her problems. Karen and I told her about Jesus and that He loved her very much. She hugged us and thanked us for caring about her.

We saw Shani only a few times after that. Each time we talked about her life and about Jesus. All too soon, she went back to Chicago. We pray for Shani every night. We ask God to finish the work He began in her. We know He will.

Lord, Make Me a Blessing to Someone Today

We have had many encounters with people like the two above. Each one is different. What is unique about each is that Jesus shows us who is open, who is hungry for Him, and who needs Him. On a typical day, you may pass dozens, even hundreds of people. But Jesus knows what each one needs. And, if you are willing, He will use you to touch their lives with what He has for them.

If you pray, "Lord, make me a blessing to someone today," don't be surprised when He does. And I can almost guarantee you it won't be convenient or risk-free. But what adventures you are going to have! You don't want to miss this!

I pray this prayer every morning. Then I ask, "Jesus, who do You want me to bless? And how?" Sometimes, He answers right away. Sometimes, he answers later in the day by pointing someone out to me.

All around you people are lost, hurting – needing Jesus. Let Jesus use you to touch them.

Activation

1. Pray this prayer every day for a week and see what opportunities Jesus will bring to you: "Lord, make me a blessing to someone today."

Pray, then wait. Give Jesus time to answer your request. Some days He tells me who and how to be a blessing. Other days I go through the day looking for someone, and He prompts me who to bless.

2. Be interruptible. Expect to meet the person you will bless. It will probably be inconvenient. And you may have to take a risk. Do it anyway.

3. Journal your experiences. Share them with friends. This is even more fun and encouraging when you are doing it with others.

4. After seven days, read your journal. Is this a life you want to live?

Day 30 Jesus Calls, "Bring My People Back to Me."

Connecting Hearts

Saturday, June 9, 2018, I was watching a movie when God spoke to me. "Bring My people back to Me." I turned the movie off and asked God what He meant.

He said, "Call people. Show them the way. To Me, not a belief, a leader or an organization. To Me." This book is in response to that call. God wants you back. He wants you to be close to Him, to know Him, and to love Him the way He loves you.

Jesus came to reconnect our hearts to Father God. God gives us the ministry of heart connection. Most translations use "reconciliation" to describe the work God has given us. Reconcile means **to reestablish a close relationship**, e.g., friendship. God asks us to bring His people back into a close relationship with Him. Heart connection.

> This is the wonderful message he has given us to tell others. We are Christ's ambassadors. God is using us to speak to you: **we beg you, as though Christ himself were here pleading with you, receive the love he offers you—be reconciled to God.** For God took the sinless Christ and poured into him our sins. Then, in exchange, he poured God's goodness into us!
> 2 Corinthians 5:19-21 (TLB)

1. Pray Them Home

When you pray for others, you have a stake in their lives. You can't sit back, detached, and uncaring. Praying for someone makes you root for them. You feel their pain. You rejoice in their joy. You come to love them. Nothing connects our hearts with people like praying for them. The same is true when we pray for nations.

Maybe that's why we are told to pray for everyone – even our enemies. The first and greatest command of Christianity is to love God. The second is to love people as we love ourselves.

> "Teacher, which is the most important commandment in the law of Moses?"
> Jesus replied, "'You must love the Lord your God with all your heart, all your soul, and all your mind.' This is the first and greatest commandment. A second is equally important: 'Love your neighbor as yourself.'
> Matthew 22:36-38 (NLT)

Prayer is going to God to receive His love for someone and then praying that love into their lives. Faith works in love.

> For [if we are] in Christ Jesus neither circumcision nor uncircumcision means anything, but only faith activated and expressed and working through love.
> Galatians 5:6 (AMP)

Prayer, then, is using our faith to connect people to God's love.

There is power in persistent prayer. We pray until we overcome. Old timers called this "praying through to peace." And that's still what works. We pray until we have God's assurance that our prayers have been answered. That assurance is often a gentle, loving peace. Then we stand firm, knowing it will happen. Don't worry about delays after you have an answer. Stand firm.

What should I Pray?

Ask this question: *"What is keeping them from Jesus?"*

a. They can't see the truth.

2 Corinthians 3:14 says a veil that has been placed over people's eyes. The veil is lifted only by Christ.

> The god of this age has blinded the minds of unbelievers so that they cannot see the light of the gospel that displays the glory of Christ, who is the image of God.
> 2 Corinthians 4:4 (NLT)

People literally can't see the truth! In Jesus name, pray He will open their eyes and unstop their ears, that they may see and hear the truth. Remove the veil the devil has placed over their eyes.

b. The devil has strongholds in the minds of people.

We need to set them free, so they can receive the Gospel in their hearts. Day 16 Jesus Calls, "Drive Out the Inhabitants in Your Land" talks about the strongholds of false beliefs and pride and how to pray to tear down these strongholds in the lives of people.

c. Ask Jesus How to Pray

Jesus knows exactly what each of us need to be open to the life He offers. Ask Him how to pray specifically for people, and He will show you.

2. Introduce Jesus to the people you care about.

If you see Christianity as a belief system, you'll ask yourself, "How can I convince Uncle Bob to believe this?" And you'll start listing reasons, arguments to convince Uncle Bob. That approach leads to arguments and all kinds of nonsense. If you have a relationship with Jesus, then you will say: "Uncle Bob, I have someone I'd like you to know. He's helping me." And you'll tell Uncle Bob about your experiences with Jesus.

> But how can they call on him to save them unless they believe in him? And how can they believe in him if they have never heard about him? And how can they hear about him unless someone tells them?
> Romans 10:14 (NLT)

I can't tell you how many times people in China told me, "There's something different about you. What is it?" I'm not bragging. It wasn't me they saw. Jesus lives in me, and people notice. That's true of you too.

> Your heart should be holy and set apart for the Lord God. **Always be ready to tell everyone who asks you why you believe as you do.** Be gentle as you speak and show respect. Keep your heart telling you that you have done what is right. If men speak against you, they will be ashamed when they see the good way you have lived as a Christian.
> 1 Peter 3:15-16 (NLV)

It's important for you to be ready to introduce them to Jesus. Just tell them how you met Jesus. Then tell them what Jesus has done for you.

Surprise Sithole lived in the remote village of Cachote in
Mozambique. He was the son of a witch doctor. When
he was fifteen, he heard a voice in the night. "Get out
of the house. If you do not leave, you will die." After
an internal struggle, he did leave. His whole family was
murdered. He wandered in the jungle for two weeks
until he came to a strange village. A man was waiting
for him. The man said God told him Surprise would
come. The man fed him and led him to Jesus. God called
Surprise to preach the gospel. He had no Bible. John
3:16 was the only verse he knew. He went anyway. He
planted several churches with a general knowledge of
Jesus and one Bible verse.[16]

If Surprise Sithole could plant churches with one verse
and a few stories, you and I can introduce people we
love to the Son of God who loves them. It's personal.
You aren't convincing people to believe what you
believe. You are introducing them to your best friend.

3. **Love Them Home**

> Don't you see how wonderfully kind, tolerant,
> and patient God is with you? Does this mean
> nothing to you? Can't you see that **his kindness
> is intended to turn you from your sin**?
> Romans 2:4 (NLT)
> We love because God loved us first.
> 1 John 4:19 (CEV)

When I was an alcoholic, I came to hate myself for who
I had become and my inability to break free from my
addiction. God used a dear friend to confront me gently.

---

[16] Read *Voice in the Night: The True Story of a Man and the
Miracles That Are Changing Africa,* Surprise Sithole, 2012

I didn't feel condemned. I was ashamed and guilty at first. But then I realized my Christian friend knew my dark secret - and cared about me anyway. It was healing to finally be able to talk about it.

That is how God leads us to repentance. He doesn't scare us into it. He doesn't condemn or guilt trip us. No one has to tell you what's wrong with you. You know, just as I knew. God convicts and offers hope. Jesus has a better life for you.

I dared to hope. I dared to believe I could break free from my addiction. I wasn't ready to give my life to Jesus yet, but I thought that Jesus would help me. I stopped drinking that day. It was a long, painful process, but I NEVER went back. That was over 30 years ago.

Jesus wants you and I to touch the world with His redeeming, transforming love. After I became a Christian, I realized that dozens, maybe hundreds of Christians, had lovingly touched me over the years. A few months ago, I heard the Lord say that He gives each of us the ministry of nudges. I like that. That is something you and I can do no matter where we are or what we're doing: touch people with Jesus' love. Nudges.

Activation

Pray-Share-Love

Create a simple prayer Journal. Make a short list. Start with a handful of people you really love. Write their names in the journal. Begin to **Pray-Share-Love** these people. Record what you do every day and God's answers to your prayers. Let Jesus lead you. And know this is God's heart, "Bring My people back to Me."

Postscript

Saul, the murderer and enemy of Christians, had an encounter with Jesus that turned his life around. Saul became Paul. Paul came to Christ late in life, but still fulfilled God's plan for his life. Like Paul, I pray you will be able to say:

> I have fought the good fight, I have finished the race, I have kept the faith. Now there is in store for me the crown of righteousness, which the Lord, the righteous Judge, will award to me on that day—and not only to me but also to all who have longed for his appearing.
>
> 2 Timothy 4:7-8 (NIV)

Run with all your might. Run with purpose. Run in God's power, wisdom and strength. Run with Jesus at your side.

Dave

PSS.

If this book was of value to you, would you please write a review on Amazon or Goodreads so others can find it. Thank you so much!

To find the next devotional in this series go to www.davemilford.com .

Made in the USA
Monee, IL
02 July 2020

35356418R00125